Project AIR FORCE

THE CONFLICT OVER KOSOVO

T0195514

WHY MILOSEVIC DECIDED TO SETTLE WHEN HE DID

STEPHEN T. HOSMER

Prepared for the
UNITED STATES AIR FORCE

RAND

The research reported here was sponsored by the United States Air Force under Contract F49642-01-C-0003. Further information may be obtained from the Strategic Planning Division, Directorate of Plans, Hq USAF.

Library of Congress Cataloging-in-Publication Data

Hosmer, Stephen T.
   The conflict over Kosovo : why Milosevic decided to settle when he did /
Stephen T. Hosmer.
      p. cm.
   MR-1351
   Includes bibliographical references.
   ISBN 0-8330-3003-5
   1. Kosovo (Serbia)—History—Civil War, 1998– 2. Miloćeviâ, Slobodan, 1941–
I. Title.

DR2087 .H67 2001
949.7103—dc21

                                                                    2001031973

RAND is a nonprofit institution that helps improve policy and decisionmaking through research and analysis. RAND® is a registered trademark. RAND's publications do not necessarily reflect the opinions or policies of its research sponsors.

Published 2001 by RAND
1700 Main Street, P.O. Box 2138, Santa Monica, CA 90407-2138
1200 South Hayes Street, Arlington, VA 22202-5050
201 North Craig Street, Suite 102, Pittsburgh, PA 15213-1516
RAND URL: http://www.rand.org/
To order RAND documents or to obtain additional information,
contact Distribution Services: Telephone: (310) 451-7002;
Fax: (310) 451-6915; Internet: order@rand.org

Since the end of the Cold War a decade ago, the armed forces of the United States have been committed to protracted, large-scale combat operations only twice: Operation Desert Storm in 1991 and Operation Allied Force in 1999. In both conflicts, U.S. and allied air operations played a key role in securing allied war aims with minimal friendly casualties. Because U.S. military and civilian leaders will also want to conclude future conflicts at minimal cost, it is important that they understand the circumstances and operational effects that were instrumental in producing the successful outcomes of the past.

This book examines the reasons Slobodan Milosevic decided on June 3, 1999, to accept NATO's conditions for terminating the conflict over Kosovo. Among other issues, the study analyzes (1) the assumptions and other calculations that underlay Milosevic's initial decision to defy NATO's demands with regard to Kosovo, and (2) the political, economic, and military developments and pressures and the resulting expectations and concerns that most heavily influenced his subsequent decision to come to terms. Because bombing was the primary instrument used by the NATO allies, particular attention is necessarily given to identifying and assessing its different coercive effects on the Serb population and leadership.

The book should be of interest to national security officials, military commanders, and other persons responsible for the development of U.S. military capabilities, the planning and conduct of U.S. military operations, and the formulation of strategies for bringing U.S. power to bear in the service of U.S. national interests.

The research, which was part of a larger RAND Project AIR FORCE study of Operation Allied Force, was conducted within the Strategy and Doctrine Program of Project AIR FORCE and was sponsored by the Commander, United States Air Forces in Europe, and the Director of Strategic Planning, Headquarters, United States Air Force. Research was completed in March 2001. Comments are welcome and may be addressed either to the author or to the Strategy and Doctrine Program director, Edward R. Harshberger.

Other documents published in this series currently include the following:

MR-1279-AF, *Command and Control and Battle Management: Experiences from the Air War Over Serbia*, James E. Schneider, Myron Hura, Gary McLeod (Government publication; not releasable to the general public)

MR-1326-AF, *Aircraft Weapon Employment in Operation Allied Force*, William Stanley, Carl Rhodes, Robert Uy, Sherrill Lingel (Government publication; not releasable to the general public)

MR-1391-AF, *European Contributions to Operation Allied Force: Implications for Transatlantic Cooperation*, John E. Peters, Stuart Johnson, Nora Bensahel, Timothy Liston, Traci Williams

DB-332-AF, *Aircraft Survivability in Operation Allied Force*, William Stanley, Sherrill Lingel, Carl Rhodes, Jody Jacobs, Robert Uy (Government publication; not releasable to the general public)

Topics examined in series documents nearing completion include:

- Supporting Expeditionary Aerospace Forces: Lessons from the Air War Over Serbia

- A Strategic and Operational Assessment of NATO's Air War for Kosovo

- Lessons Learned from Operation Allied Force Tanker Operations

PROJECT AIR FORCE

Project AIR FORCE, a division of RAND, is the Air Force federally funded research and development center (FFRDC) for studies and analysis. It provides the Air Force with independent analyses of policy alternatives affecting the development, employment, combat readiness, and support of current and future aerospace forces. Research is carried out in four programs: Aerospace Force Development; Manpower, Personnel, and Training; Resource Management; and Strategy and Doctrine.

CONTENTS

FIGURE

This report examines two questions relating to Slobodan Milosevic's decision on June 3, 1999, to accept NATO's terms for settling the conflict over Kosovo: first, why he did not decide to settle earlier—say, by signing the Rambouillet Agreement or coming to terms after a few days of bombing, as many allied leaders expected he would—and second, why he did not attempt to hold out even longer, as most NATO leaders feared he would.

MILOSEVIC ASSUMED ACCEPTING RAMBOUILLET TERMS MIGHT ENDANGER HIS RULE

One likely reason Milosevic did not capitulate early on was that he thought it too dangerous to do so. The proximate cause for the NATO bombing that began on March 24, 1999, was Milosevic's refusal to sign the Rambouillet Agreement, which he and other Serbs opposed primarily because it would have ended the Serb hegemony in Kosovo. The agreement would have severely restricted Serbia's military and police presence in the province and empowered NATO to constitute and lead a military force to help keep the peace. Serbs also believed the Rambouillet terms would have jeopardized Serbia's ultimate sovereignty over Kosovo by permitting the province's future to be determined by a referendum—a vote they knew the Kosovo Albanians seeking independence surely would have won. Although the Belgrade leaders did not cite them at the time as reasons for their refusal to sign the agreement, other provisions of the Rambouillet Agreement also seriously infringed on their nation's sovereignty by according NATO forces access, billeting, and utilization rights throughout the entirety of the Federal Republic of Yugoslavia (FRY).

Milosevic might have endangered his continued rule had he accepted Rambouillet's terms without a fight or a prior consensus to yield on the part of the Serbian populace. The Serbian people were strongly attached to Kosovo as the cradle of their ancient culture, and Milosevic's rise to power and credibility as a nationalist leader stemmed largely from his promotion of Serb hegemony in the province. Moreover, Milosevic had relied on Kosovo as a means to bolster his sagging political position within Serbia, exploiting the issue to raise nationalist passions, mobilize public support, and distract the people from the other serious problems plaguing Serbia.

MILOSEVIC ASSUMED THE BOMBING WOULD BE LIMITED AND THAT HE COULD GET BETTER TERMS BY HOLDING FIRM

While Milosevic expected to be bombed if he refused to sign the Rambouillet Agreement, his intelligence sources and perceptions of recent U.S. and NATO behavior probably encouraged him to believe that any NATO air strikes would be of limited duration and severity. But even if the bombing proved more costly than expected, Milosevic apparently assumed that sufficient countervailing pressures would eventually come to bear on NATO to cause the allies to terminate the bombing and agree to interim arrangements for Kosovo that were more acceptable to Belgrade.

Milosevic assumed that large-scale ethnic cleansing of Kosovo would present NATO with *faits accomplis* by eliminating the Kosovo Liberation Army (KLA) as a factor in any future settlement and by permanently changing Kosovo's ethnic balance. Most important, he expected the ethnic cleansing to show the bombing to be counterproductive in that it appeared to be intensifying rather than preventing the acute humanitarian crisis that NATO had aimed to forestall. Milosevic also expected Serb civilian casualties and NATO pilot losses from the bombing to turn the NATO publics against the war and thereby undermine Alliance unity and resolve. Finally, he assumed that Russia would steadfastly support Serbia's position and apply pressure on NATO to terminate the bombing.

MILOSEVIC EVENTUALLY REALIZED THAT HIS HOPED-FOR LEVERAGE ON NATO HAD EVAPORATED

While a number of weeks were to pass before all of these assumptions would be fully tested, in the end, none bore out. Milosevic's decision to push some 700,000 refugees into Macedonia and Albania turned out to be a major blunder. The horror of the ethnic cleansing hardened NATO's terms for war termination and strengthened the resolve of the NATO governments to continue the bombing despite the toll of civilian casualties involved. The expectations that FRY military forces would impose costs on NATO by downing large numbers of NATO aircraft and gain bargaining leverage for Belgrade by capturing allied pilots were also unrealized.

Milosevic's assumption that he could count on Russia's continued backing also proved misguided. While Russian public opinion strongly supported Serbia, Yeltsin believed that a protraction or escalation of the conflict would act against Russia's fundamental economic and other interests in maintaining good relations with the West. NATO's steadfastness and Moscow's apparent belief that a NATO ground invasion was looming eventually led Yeltsin to break ranks with Belgrade and agree to endorse NATO's key bottom-line demands for war termination, namely that all Serb forces be withdrawn from Kosovo and that a NATO-led military presence in Kosovo with "substantial" NATO participation be introduced to keep the peace.

THE BOMBING PRODUCED A POLITICAL CLIMATE CONDUCIVE TO CONCESSIONS

The initial popular response to the bombing was one of patriotic defiance: The Serbian people rallied around the flag (and Milosevic) and supported the Belgrade government's refusal to yield on Kosovo. After a month or so of bombing, however, the popular mood began to change: People became increasingly war weary, concerned about their daily survival, and desirous that the bombing end. The changes in popular attitudes were conditioned by three effects of the bombing: (1) the immediate physical hardships it caused individual Serbian citizens, (2) the fears—exacerbated by constant air raid alerts—it generated among the public about their own safety and that of their loved ones, and (3) the anxieties it engendered among the public about the vicissitudes they were likely to face in the future. These concerns intensified as the bombing became prolonged and increasingly embraced a larger array of infrastructure targets that directly affected the public, such as Serbia's bridges and electric power grids.

The change in public mood was accompanied by calls from opposition party leaders and elected officials for a negotiated settlement. The mounting popular support for a settlement that would end the bombing apparently persuaded Milosevic that he could now make concessions that might have cost him his power before the air attacks began. Indeed, when the conflict ended, there were no demonstrations against the concessions made by the Belgrade regime, even by the radical nationalists who had vowed never to allow foreign troops to enter Kosovo.

THE BOMBING GENERATED GROWING PRESSURES WITHIN THE REGIME FOR COMPROMISE

Most Pressure Arose from Damage to Serbia's Economy and "Dual-Use" Infrastructure

By the beginning of June, Milosevic was reportedly under increasing pressure—particularly from his closest associates—to agree to a settlement that would halt the bombing. Much of the impulse for this pressure seems to have resulted from NATO attacks on six types of largely "dual-use" infrastructure targets: command, control, and communication (C^3), electric power, industrial plant, leadership, lines of communication (LOCs), and petroleum, oil, and lubricant (POL) facilities—the bulk of which were located in Serbia, the area of transcending political importance to Milosevic and his colleagues.

The air attacks on infrastructure targets, along with the international embargoes and other sanctions the allies imposed, were causing significant additional damage to a Serbian economy that was already in serious decline. Estimates of the costs of repairing the physical destruction already experienced in Serbia ranged in the tens of billions of U.S. dollars, a daunting amount for a pariah government bereft of foreign reserves. The bombing had also greatly increased unemployment in Serbia, including that among the blue-collar workers who had traditionally supported Milosevic and his Socialist Party. Those in the leadership pressing for war termination undoubtedly worried that the dismal economic conditions—including the government's lack of funds to pay pensioners and troops—and the increasing joblessness were creating the potential for widespread future unrest in Serbia, an unrest that in time might grow to a magnitude that would topple the regime.

The bombing was also imposing psychological and physical hardships on the ruling elite. The trauma caused by frequent and prolonged air raid warnings and the deprivations caused by the electric power blackouts in Belgrade undoubtedly affected the families of many persons connected to the regime. The air attacks were also destroying assets owned by the ruling elite, including the manufacturing facilities of Milosevic "cronies" who were undoubtedly eager to get the bombing stopped.

ATTACKS ON PURELY MILITARY TARGETS PROBABLY DID NOT PROVIDE A MAJOR SOURCE OF PRESSURE

Even though purely military targets were the primary focus of the NATO air campaign and accounted for the vast majority of weapons expended, the destruction and damage to military targets probably did not generate the major pressure for war termination. The effects of the losses in military infrastructure caused by the bombing were more long term than immediate. Except for the FRY air force, which lost a significant percentage of its frontline aircraft, the NATO attacks did not greatly diminish the FRY's combat structure. Most of the purely military facilities that were struck were probably empty of personnel and equipment when hit, and only a portion of the FRY's ground force structure was actually attacked.

Furthermore, those deployed force elements that NATO attempted to attack—the tanks, armored personnel carriers (APCs), and artillery/mortars of the Third Army and the Ministry of Internal Affairs Police Forces (MUP) in Kosovo—often escaped destruction because NATO aircraft found it difficult to locate, positively identify, and promptly strike such mobile targets. The actual results of the air attacks on the Serb armor and artillery deployed in Kosovo are in dis-

pute. However, even if one assumed that all the equipment identi-
fied in the Kosovo Strike Assessment as having received a "successful
hit" proved to be beyond repair, the amount of armor and artillery
lost to NATO air attacks still would constitute only a small percentage
of the FRY's total armor and artillery inventories.

While the personnel losses in the Yugoslav Army (VJ) and MUP
caused by the bombing and ground engagements with the KLA were
probably modest, concerns about casualties among the troops deployed in Kosovo prompted antiwar protests in several south-central
Serbian towns. These antiwar demonstrations were undoubtedly
worrisome to the Belgrade regime in that they occurred in areas
where Milosevic's Socialist Party had traditionally enjoyed strong
popular support.

The NATO air operations in Kosovo limited the potential combat effectiveness of the Third Army—particularly with respect to counter-
ing a future NATO ground invasion—by forcing VJ units to disperse
and avoid large-scale operations. However, this dispersed and buttoned-up posture did not prevent VJ and MUP forces from carrying
out—albeit with some difficulty—their immediate missions of (1)
conducting ethnic cleansing, (2) rooting out and suppressing the KLA
elements in Kosovo, (3) preventing the infiltration of KLA forces from
Albania, and (4) strengthening Kosovo's physical defenses against invasion.

Neither the limited losses in ground combat capability the FRY suffered as a result of the NATO bombing nor the purported
"resurgence" of the KLA military threat to Serb forces in Kosovo appears to have importantly influenced Milosevic's decision to come to
terms. The reporting that Milosevic received from his military commander in Kosovo apparently continued to be upbeat throughout
the war. Moreover, Serb officials, when discussing the decision to
yield, mention neither the attrition of the FRY's military forces nor
the supposed deterioration of the military balance in Kosovo as major reasons for Belgrade's capitulation.

MILOSEVIC EXPECTED UNCONSTRAINED BOMBING IF NATO'S TERMS WERE REJECTED

According to Milosevic's own testimony and the contemporary statements of senior FRY officials and close Milosevic associates, the key reason Milosevic agreed to accept NATO's terms was his fear of the bombing that would follow if he refused. Milosevic and his colleagues apparently believed that the allies, with Russia's acquiescence, had presented Serbia with an ultimatum on June 2 and that NATO was poised to launch a "fierce" and unconstrained bombing campaign if its terms were rejected. As Milosevic described it, had the Serbs rejected an agreement that had been endorsed by Russia—a reputed defender of Serb interests—they would have been dismissed as a people "with whom you cannot reason in any way," and NATO would have been able to use the rejection as a license to engage in "even more massive bombing" at the cost "of a great number of lives."

The Serb leaders anticipated that the future NATO attacks would focus heavily on Belgrade and would prove far more destructive than the bombing they had experienced to date. Indeed, they were apparently convinced that NATO was prepared to demolish Serbia's entire infrastructure—including its remaining bridges, electric power facilities, telephone systems, and factories—and concluded that they had no choice but to accede to NATO's demands to forestall such unacceptable damage.

Serb leaders probably found the threat of unconstrained bombing credible because they: (1) observed an escalating pattern to recent NATO air attacks, (2) saw evidence that NATO was accumulating aircraft and bases for a greatly expanded air campaign, (3) knew NATO leaders had warned of devastating attacks, (4) erroneously believed NATO to be already purposely attacking civilian targets, and (5) heard the Russian envoy, Viktor Chernomyrdin, predicting massive devastation if the conflict continued.

Milosevic had every reason to contemplate the prospect of unconstrained bombing with trepidation. He recognized that Serbia had no defense against air attacks on fixed targets and realized that the weather for bombing was improving. He further knew that if there were no containment and reconstitution of the damage being inflicted on Serbia, the coming winter would greatly magnify the hardships for the Serbian people. The prospect of a prolonged denial of electric power was undoubtedly the most worrisome contingency, as it would have threatened the heating of 75 percent of Serbian homes, shut down the country's water supply and sewage services, and seriously impaired the storage, preparation, and processing of food.

Milosevic had reason to doubt that the Serb public would have passively accepted such deprivation for long once the frigid Balkan winter set in. He almost certainly realized that subjecting Serbia to further months of unconstrained bombing risked decisively weakening his rule and that he could best survive in power only if he preserved at least a partially stable and functioning country. Thus, he decided to come to terms "to salvage what could be salvaged, that being his power in Serbia."

MILOSEVIC PROBABLY ALSO WORRIED ABOUT THE THREAT OF A FUTURE INVASION

The increasing talk of an eventual NATO ground invasion was probably another, albeit lesser, factor in Milosevic's decision. Serb military leaders had from the outset been sensitive to the possibility that NATO might eventually invade the FRY and had taken measures to strengthen their land defenses. However, the Serb leaders probably realized that there was as yet no consensus within NATO for an invasion and were aware that NATO did not yet have sufficient troops within the theater to conduct a ground campaign. According to Western estimates, it would have taken two to three months to deploy an adequate invasion force to the area.

Even if an invasion was not imminent, the indicators that a ground attack was being considered probably worried Milosevic. He had been told by the Russians that an invasion was coming and was no doubt aware of the increasing discussion of a ground option in Washington and some other NATO capitals. It is likely that Milosevic would have found the prospect of an invasion extremely threatening, for he would have worried that any NATO ground operation might not be limited to Kosovo but could move on Belgrade and directly endanger his personal safety and freedom. As of June 2, however, Milosevic appeared clearly more concerned about the threat to his power from an intensified NATO bombing campaign than about the possible consequence of a still-distant invasion.

NATO'S FINAL TERMS PROVIDED MILOSEVIC WITH SOME MINIMAL POLITICAL COVER

Finally, Milosevic acceded to NATO's demands because he was convinced that NATO's terms were unlikely to improve and realized that the terms being offered provided him with some political cover. The final settlement embodied in Security Council Resolution 1244 satisfied the conditions NATO had laid down for a cessation of the bombing. In certain respects, such as the requirements governing the withdrawal of VJ and MUP forces from Kosovo, the terms provided in Resolution 1244 were less favorable to Belgrade than the terms contained in the Rambouillet Agreement.

However, Serb leaders could portray other settlement provisions as improvements over the Rambouillet terms: NATO forces were now accorded access only to Kosovo; there was no longer a suggestion that Kosovo's future might be determined, even in part, by a referendum; and the United Nations, rather than the Organization for Security and Cooperation in Europe (OSCE), was now assigned responsibility for controlling the implementation of the international civil presence in Kosovo. Milosevic would claim a victory of sorts by asserting that the United Nations had now become the guarantor of the FRY's sovereignty and territorial integrity and that possible independence for Kosovo had now become a "closed" issue.

But Milosevic could not mask the facts that the FRY could no longer protect the Serbs in Kosovo, the majority of whom were already beginning to flee to Serbia; that NATO commanded and controlled the armed presence in Kosovo and provided the bulk of its forces; and that the Kosovo Albanians were likely to govern Kosovo in the manner of an independent, sovereign state.

CONCLUDING OBSERVATIONS

Air Power's Contributions Were Crucial

It was the cumulative effect of NATO air power that most influenced Milosevic's eventual decision to come to terms. Air power made three crucial contributions: (1) the bombing created a political climate within Serbia conducive to concessions, (2) the bombing, as it intensified, stimulated a growing interest on the part of Milosevic and his associates to end the conflict, and (3) the perception that any future bombing would be unconstrained made a settlement seem imperative. Air power also delivered crucial humanitarian support when it was badly needed and provided the spur to prevent Serb stalling and backsliding during the military-technical negotiations that preceded the June 10 cease-fire.

NATO's air operations were conducted in a manner that successfully confounded Milosevic's attempts to erode support for the war within the allied countries. The measures NATO leaders adopted to avoid allied KIAs and POWs and to hold down enemy civilian casualties and collateral damage were crucial to limiting active opposition to the war among important wavering domestic constituencies, such as the members of the Green Party in Germany.

The Conditions Prompting the Serbs to Settle Were Also Evident in Other Conflicts

Commentators have suggested that Operation Allied Force lies outside the mainstream of the U.S. experience with the coercive use of air power in that it was conducted in the absence of a simultaneous ground battle. Some commentators even contended that this was the "first time" air attacks had played a crucial role in persuading enemy decisionmakers to come to terms. Contrary to such assertions, the evidence suggests that the military pressures and other conditions that forced Milosevic to come to terms generally paralleled the military pressures and conditions that had compelled enemy leaders in other past conflicts to capitulate or agree to negotiated settlements acceptable to the United States.

Analyses of past conflicts have shown that air attacks or threatened air attacks have helped persuade enemy decisionmakers to terminate conflicts on terms acceptable to the United States when the enemy leaders perceived that:

- their military forces no longer possessed a viable, near-term offensive option and faced stalemate or eventual defeat on the battlefield

- they were unlikely to get better peace terms if they prolonged the fighting

- they had no prospect of mounting an effective defense against the air attacks or of compelling a stop to the coercive bombing

- the cost of the damage from future air attacks was likely to significantly outweigh the costs of the concessions the United States and its allies were demanding.

All these conditions prevailed at the time air attacks or the threat of air attacks helped force war termination with Japan in 1945, Korea in 1953, Vietnam in 1973, Iraq in 1991, the Bosnian Serbs in 1995, and Serbia in 1999. In each instance, it was more the damage that the enemy decisionmakers feared would be inflicted in the future than the damage they had already absorbed that drove the enemy leaders to a settlement.

Milosevic's Decision to Yield Depended on Developments That Took Time to Mature

It has been suggested that a more robust bombing of infrastructure targets in Belgrade at the outset of the conflict would have produced success within a quarter to a third of the (11-week) period it actually took to bring Milosevic to terms. While persuasive arguments can be made that going "downtown" from the outset could have shortened the war, it is by no means certain that this would have been the case to the extent predicted.

Milosevic's decision to yield depended in part on developments that took time to mature, such as Russia's eventual decision to agree to NATO's settlement terms. Time was also required for Milosevic to become disabused of his expectations that the humanitarian crisis caused by ethnic cleansing and the accumulating civilian casualties caused by the bombing would eventually erode NATO's resolve to continue the air campaign. It should also be recalled that an important ingredient of the war weariness that eventually invaded the Serbian public was the cumulative stress caused by daily air raid alerts. It is also unclear whether going "downtown" immediately might have served to dampen rather than intensify Serb fears of NATO escalation. Attacking Belgrade heavily from the outset might have had the perverse effect of "killing the hostage"—that is, causing enough damage to convince the Serb leaders that they had little to lose by holding out longer.

Whatever its potential coercive effects, attacking Belgrade in a robust manner at the outset of the war was never a feasible option. The NATO allies had resorted to bombing only reluctantly and hoped to succeed with limited force. The allies agreed to attack sensitive targets, such as the facilities providing electric power to Belgrade, only when it became apparent that lesser measures would not suffice to bring about a settlement.

NATO and Serb Leaders Perceived Strategic Bombing Differently

There was a striking incongruity between Serb and NATO perceptions of the air campaign. Even though NATO commanders accepted the need to minimize civilian casualties and collateral damage, they nevertheless felt that their air operations were overly constrained. They believed the efficiency and potential effectiveness of their air attacks were significantly hindered by the slow release or outright denial of lucrative strategic targets, particularly in Belgrade, and by the increasingly tight rules of engagement (ROEs) that were imposed after NATO bombing errors.

The Serb view of the NATO air campaign was entirely different. The Serbs perceived NATO's attacks to be intentionally directed at civilian as well as military targets. Most important, Milosevic and his colleagues apparently believed that NATO had both the intent and the freedom of action to destroy their country's entire infrastructure if need be. This distorted perception of the allied threat greatly benefited NATO when it came to persuading Milosevic to accept its terms for war termination—for had the Serb perception of NATO's freedom of action to engage in unconstrained bombing more closely paralleled the views of the NATO commanders, the conflict might have continued longer.

Capabilities to Coerce Future Adversary Leaders Must be Maintained

While not a template for future military operations, the NATO air campaign was conducted under constraints that are likely to be present in future conflicts. Operation Allied Force provides insights about the capabilities and freedom of action that U.S. and allied forces may need to maximize the coercive effects of air power in conflict situations similar to that encountered in Kosovo.

Improve Capabilities to Attack Dispersed and Hidden Forces. NATO's attempts to "systematically" and "progressively" destroy the FRY's military forces and thereby pressure Milosevic to come to terms proved largely unsuccessful. The Serbs were able to preserve intact the vast bulk of their ground forces by dispersing them before the bombing began and by making extensive use of concealment, camouflage, and hardened underground shelters. They were also able to shield their forces from attack by locating them among civilian facilities and populations. It can be assumed that future adversaries will resort to similar measures to limit the destructive effects of friendly air power on their ground forces when battlefield situations so permit.

To counter such tactics, the United States and its allies must seek to develop sensors, surveillance and reconnaissance platforms, target processing and dynamic control measures, weapon systems, and concepts of operation that will improve their capabilities to attack enemy armored and artillery forces when such forces are widely dispersed, hidden under foliage, or located in civilian settings. To minimize civilian casualties and collateral damage, extremely accurate low-yield munitions will be required to attack enemy military forces located in or near civilian structures. Special munitions will also be required to effectively attack enemy leadership and C^3 facilities that are located deep underground.

Whenever feasible, allied air campaigns against enemy ground forces should be accompanied by the credible threat of an allied ground attack. The presence of an allied ground threat will cause enemy forces to concentrate and thereby become rich targets for air attack. In addition, the presence of an allied ground threat will heighten the enemy leaders' concerns that their continued resistance might eventually invite their overthrow and punishment by allied invasion forces.

Preserve Option to Attack "Dual-Use" Infrastructure Targets. In the Kosovo conflict, it was the attacks and threat of additional attacks on "dual-use" infrastructure targets that generated the decisive pressure for war termination. However, the freedom of action to attack such targets in future conflicts could become circumscribed because of U.S. and allied leaders' concerns about being prosecuted as "war criminals" or an inability to attack such targets without significant civilian casualties.

One of the fundamental concerns voiced about the Rome Treaty creating the International Criminal Court (ICC) is that it would expose U.S. civilian and military leaders and other personnel who were acting within the authority of the U.S. government to unwarranted prosecution. Attacks on "dual-use" military targets may pose particular risk of legal sanction in that the military utility and therefore the legitimacy of a particular target can differ with the eye of the beholder.

Attacks or threats of attacks on "dual-use" military targets may be the most effective way—and in some instances the only feasible way—to coerce enemy decisionmakers to terminate conflicts and crises rapidly, on terms acceptable to the United States. Speedy war termination may ultimately save enemy as well as friendly lives. It is therefore important that the United States not assume binding international obligations that could subject U.S. civilian and military leaders and other personnel to prosecution for attacking targets that responsible U.S. legal authorities have certified to be legitimate military targets. Otherwise, U.S. civilian officials and war fighters may be deterred from prosecuting effective air campaigns because of the concern that they might be indicted and even convicted as war criminals by prosecutors and jurists who hold to a different view about the legitimacy of certain targets and who may harbor animus toward the United States. Nor should U.S. persons be allowed to be deterred from conducting their military duties by the fear that they will be prosecuted for unintended bombing errors.

But to retain the option to strike "dual-use" targets, it will also be necessary that such attacks be conducted with minimal loss of civilian life and other unintended damage. Military leaders must ensure that U.S. and allied forces possess the precision strike capabilities, training, target intelligence, situational awareness, ROEs, and concepts of operation that will enable those forces to attack "dual-use" as well as other targets with minimal civilian casualties and collateral damage. These capabilities will be needed not only to comply with the laws of war but also to maintain the political support that will be required to sustain U.S. and allied military interventions, particularly when less than vital national interests are at stake. In Operation Allied Force, the ROEs and other actions the allies adopted to hold down civilian casualties were a key factor in sustaining NATO's freedom of action to prosecute the conflict over Kosovo to its successful conclusion.

ACKNOWLEDGMENTS

I wish to express my indebtedness and gratitude to RAND colleagues who contributed to this study: David Ochmanek, the study's project leader, who helped importantly with the data collection and provided valuable support and analytical insights throughout the course of the research, and Robert Mullins, who expertly collected and distilled source materials and analyzed key target attack data. I also want to thank Robert Hunter and Bruce Nardulli for their careful reading of the manuscript and thoughtful comments, criticisms, and suggestions.

ACRONYMS

AAA	Antiaircraft artillery
ACTORD	Activation order
APC	Armored personnel carrier
AWOS	Air War over Serbia
BDA	Bomb damage assessment
C^3	Command, control, and communication
CSAR	Combat search and rescue
DMPI	Desired mean point of impact
DSP	Defense Support Program
EU	European Union
FAC	Forward air controller
FRY	Federal Republic of Yugoslavia
GAO	General Accounting Office
HARM	High-speed antiradiation missile
IAD	Integrated air defense
ICC	International Criminal Court

ICTY	International Criminal Tribunal for the Former Yugoslavia
IDP	Internally displaced person
IMF	International monetary fund
IR	Infrared
JULL	Yugoslav United Left Party
KFOR	Kosovo Force
KIA	Killed in action
KLA	Kosovo Liberation Army
KTO	Kuwait Theater of Operations
KVM	Kosovo Verification Mission
LOC	Line of communication
MEAT	Munitions Effectiveness Assessment Team
MLRS	Multiple-launch rocket system
MUP	*Ministarstvo Unutrasnih Poslova* (Ministry of Internal Affairs) Police Forces
NAC	North Atlantic Council
NATO	North Atlantic Treaty Organization
OSCE	Organization for Security and Cooperation in Europe
POL	Petroleum, oil, and lubricant
POW	Prisoner of war
PSYOPS	Psychological operations
ROE	Rules of engagement
RTS	Radio Television Serbia

SACEUR	Supreme allied commander, Europe
SAM	Surface-to-air missile
SEAD	Suppression of enemy air defense
TRIADS	Tri-wall Aerial Delivery System
UAV	Unmanned aerial vehicle
UCK	*Ushtria Clirimtare Kosoves* (Also Kosovo Liberation Army [KLA])
USAFE	United States Air Forces in Europe
VJ	*Vojska Jugoslavije* (Yugoslav Army)
WMD	Weapons of mass destruction

Chapter One

INTRODUCTION

Slobodan Milosevic, then president of the Federal Republic of Yugoslavia (FRY), essentially agreed to settle the conflict over Kosovo on June 3, 1999, when he accepted the NATO peace terms presented to him on the previous day by Finnish president Martti Ahtisaari and Russian envoy Viktor Chernomyrdin.

This report examines two questions relating to Milosevic's decision to yield: first, why he did not decide to settle earlier—say, by signing the Rambouillet Agreement or coming to terms after a few days of bombing as many allied leaders expected he would—and second, why he did not attempt to hold out even longer, as most NATO leaders feared he would. The report weighs and analyzes the various factors that appear to have shaped Milosevic's decisionmaking

Drawing on this analysis of Milosevic's calculations concerning war termination, the report assesses the contributions of NATO's 78-day bombing campaign to the eventual settlement, demonstrates how the political-military conditions that prompted the settlement paralleled those of other conflicts, explores factors that might have hastened or slowed the timing of Milosevic's decision to come to terms, and examines the capabilities and freedom of action U.S. forces may need to maximize the coercive effects of air power in future conflicts.

Attempting to elucidate the reasoning of an authoritarian leader who shielded himself behind a screen of secrecy and propaganda is, of course, no easy task. According to those who observed him, Milosevic's decisionmaking style had several idiosyncrasies that made the FRY leader difficult to read. He was wont to gamble in his decisionmaking and prone to decide issues without adequate consultation, information, or staff support. While tactically adept, he was time and again shown to have a poor strategic grasp.[1] During negotiations, he tended to hold firm to his maximum demands, but then suddenly yield on important issues.

However, our understanding of Milosevic is aided by one overriding constant in his decision process: his propensity to weigh alternative courses of action almost entirely in terms of how they might affect his personal hold on power. The evidence suggests that Milosevic consistently viewed his options with regard to the Kosovo conflict solely through this lens of self-interest.

It is important to acknowledge that the absence of authoritative documentary evidence and in-depth oral histories from Milosevic and other key Serb officials and advisers must necessarily render any conclusions about the actual sources of Milosevic's decisions during the Kosovo crisis somewhat speculative. Even so, during the course of this research, the author has been able to derive credible and persuasive evidence about the considerations that shaped Milosevic's calculations from (1) statements made by Milosevic himself, (2) statements and published interviews of Serb and foreign military and civilian officials who directly interacted with Milosevic, (3) commentary by independent Serb analysts who claimed to have access to sources conversant with his thinking, and (4) inferences that could be drawn from Serb wartime policy and behavior, and the conditions and indicators of possible allied action that confronted Milosevic at the time of his decisions. Information about the general effects of the NATO bombing on the Serb economy and Serbian lifestyles and about Serbian attitudes toward the war was derived from opinion

---

[1]Nothing so captured Milosevic's capacity for strategic misjudgment as the calculations that led to his electoral defeat on September 24, 2000, and his subsequent forced resignation from power on October 6, 2000. As a *Washington Post* analysis described the FRY leader's thinking:

> Milosevic began his campaign this summer genuinely believing he could win the election. When he lost it, he believed he could steal it. And when he couldn't steal it, he believed—finally and desperately—that the police and the army would crush the people to keep him in power. He was wrong on all counts.

See R. Jeffrey Smith and Peter Finn, "How Milosevic Lost His Grip," *Washington Post*, October 15, 2000, pp. A1 and A30.

polls conducted in Serbia and from the reporting of numerous independent domestic and foreign correspondents who covered the conflict from inside the FRY.[2]

---

[2]As of April 12, 1999, some 947 domestic and foreign reporters had been accredited by FRY authorities to cover the war, including some 615 reporters working for foreign media. Of these, 470 were foreign citizens accredited as "special correspondents." Some 37 reporters from the United States, United Kingdom, France, and Germany were expelled at the beginning of the air campaign, but some of these were subsequently allowed to return to Yugoslavia to cover the war. See Yugoslav Army Supreme Command Headquarters—Information Service, "Foreign Correspondents in Yugoslavia," Press Center, April 12, 1999.

Part I

WHY MILOSEVIC DIDN'T SETTLE EARLIER

Chapter Two

HE ASSUMED ACCEPTING RAMBOUILLET TERMS WOULD ENDANGER HIS RULE

The immediate cause of the NATO decision to bomb the FRY on March 24, 1999, was Milosevic's refusal to sign the Rambouillet Agreement establishing peace and self-government in Kosovo. The escalation of the fighting between Serb and KLA forces in Kosovo during 1998 and the looming humanitarian crisis engendered by the Serb counterinsurgency operations that drove hundreds of thousands of Kosovo Albanians into the hills energized the NATO governments and other members of the international community to seek a restoration of peace in the province. In October 1998, Milosevic, under the threat of NATO bombing, reluctantly agreed to reduce and redeploy elements of the Serb police and military forces stationed in Kosovo and to allow 2000 unarmed Organization for Security and Cooperation in Europe (OSCE) inspectors to enter the province to verify a cessation of hostilities. However, the Serb massacre of 45 Kosovo Albanians on January 15, 1999, together with other evidence that the unarmed verification mission could not ensure compliance with the troop withdrawal agreement or stem the rising tide of violence in Kosovo, prompted the Contact Group seeking to restore peace in the province to intensify its efforts to reach a peaceful solution.[1]

---

[1]The Contact Group included representatives from the United States, the United Kingdom, France, Germany, Italy, Russia, the European Union Presidency, and the European Commission.

On January 29, the Contact Group ministers summoned the Serbian and Kosovo Albanian parties to negotiations at Rambouillet, France, to begin on February 6 under the chairmanship of the UK foreign secretary and his French counterpart. The negotiations were to define the terms of an agreement that would provide for a cease-fire, an interim peace settlement and system of self-government for Kosovo, and the deployment of an international force within Kosovo to uphold that settlement.[2]

To back up the Contact Group's action, NATO warned both the Serb and Kosovo Albanian parties on January 30 that they must respond to the summons to Rambouillet, halt the fighting, and comply with the October agreement or NATO would "take whatever measures were necessary to avert a humanitarian catastrophe."[3] Even though both parties were warned, NATO was contemplating military action only against the Serbs. Indeed, the subsequent message delivered to Milosevic was that if the Kosovo Albanians signed the Rambouillet Agreement and he did not, the FRY would be bombed.[4]

MILOSEVIC HAD MAJOR STAKES IN KOSOVO

The notion that he yield Serbia's control of Kosovo even under the duress of a NATO bombing threat was anathema to Milosevic. The FRY president had at least four important reasons for wanting to maintain Serb control and dominance within the province.

First, the vast majority of Serbs had a strong attachment to Kosovo, which they consider "the cradle of Serbia's identity and the mainspring of its ancient culture."[5] The province holds numerous

---

[2]See Memorandum by the Foreign and Commonwealth Office, "Kosovo: History of the Crisis," Select Committee on Foreign Affairs, Fourth Report, Minutes of Evidence, House of Commons, May 23, 2000, http://www.parliament.the-stationary-off.../pa/cm199900/cmselect/cmfaff/28/9111803.html.

[3]Ibid.

[4]Authority to implement the activation order (ACTORD) for air operations against the FRY was given to the NATO Secretary-General. However, it is unlikely that the Secretary General would have exercised this authority to commence the bombing unless he was confident such action had the support of the North Atlantic Council (NAC).

[5]See Dusko Doder and Louise Branson, *Milosevic, Portrait of a Tyrant*, New York: The Free Press, 1999, p. 56. For other accounts of Kosovo's history and relationship to the

shrines of the Serbian Orthodox church and artifacts of the former Serb medieval kingdom and is the site of the famous Field of Blackbirds, where the Turks vanquished the Serbs in 1389. Kosovo had assumed a "mystical importance" for many Serbs, generating memories of vanished glories that have been "kept alive in legends and folk songs on which every Serb child—including Milosevic—has been reared for the past six centuries."[6] As a consequence, Serb public opinion strongly opposed any infringement of Serb sovereignty with respect to Kosovo and supported the government's use of lethal force to suppress the Kosovo Liberation Army (KLA) "terrorists" who were attempting to wrest the province from Serbian control.

Second, Milosevic's own political persona was closely associated with the Serb ascendancy in Kosovo. Milosevic had become famous overnight in 1987, when he "legitimized the venting of Serb ethnic grievances against the Albanian majority" by promising a mob of Kosovo Serbs who had been complaining about their mistreatment by Kosovo Albanian police that "no one should dare to beat you!"[7] Milosevic clearly owed his initial rise to power in the Serbian communist party and the FRY to his exploitation of Serbian nationalist sentiments and the promotion of Serbian hegemony in Kosovo—a task he consummated in 1989 when he abolished the broad autonomy the province had enjoyed under the 1974 constitution.[8]

Third, Kosovo, from the early 1990s onward, had provided Milosevic's ruling Socialist Party with sufficient additional seats in the Serbian parliament to give it a near parliamentary majority.[9]

Serbs, see Julie A. Mertus, *Kosovo: How Myths and Truths Started a War*, Berkeley and Los Angeles: University of California Press, 1999, and Noel Malcolm, *Kosovo: A Short History*, New York: Harper Perennial, 1999.

[6]Doder and Branson, 1999, pp. 51–56.

[7]For accounts of Milosevic's April 24, 1987, meeting with Kosovo Serb demonstrators in the Pristina suburb of Kosovo Polje, see Tim Judah, *Kosovo: War and Revenge*, New Haven, CT: Yale University Press, 2000, pp. 52–53, and Doder and Branson, 1999, p. 3.

[8]*RFE/RL Balkan Report*, Vol. 2, No. 48, December 9, 1998.

[9]In the 1993 elections, which were boycotted by the Kosovo Albanians, the Socialist Party won 21 of its 123 parliamentary seats in Kosovo, leaving it just three seats short of a majority. See Eric D. Gordy, "Why Milosevic Still?" *Current History*, March 2000, p. 102.

During the 1997 parliamentary elections, the Socialist Party had again been able to pick up more than 20 seats by "stuffing ballot boxes" in Kosovo, a fraud facilitated by the Kosovo Albanian majority's continued boycott of the polls. Had the Kosovo seats been denied them, the Socialists would have held fewer seats in the Serbian parliament than the extreme nationalist Serbian Radical Party led by Vojisläv Seselj.[10]

Finally, Milosevic had continued to rely on Kosovo as a means to bolster his sagging political position within Serbia, exploiting the Kosovo issue to raise nationalist passions, mobilize public support, and distract people from the other serious problems facing Serbia.[11]

While Milosevic's manner of rule was authoritarian, depending heavily on his control of the police, media, and patronage, his power was less than absolute. He could be made to back down when faced with widespread public opposition such as that which occurred in 1997, when repeated mass protests forced him to allow the opposition parties that had won control of city governments in the 1996 elections to take office.

Milosevic had to rely on elections to extend his rule, and even though his Socialist Party had failed to receive a majority of votes in any of the elections held since 1990, it managed to maintain a majority in the Serbian parliament "through creative districting, manipulation of election returns, and a revolving cast of coalition partners."[12] For electoral support, Milosevic relied primarily on a diminishing political base of older, rural, less educated citizens, blue-collar workers, and persons with a strongly nationalist bent.[13] Polls consistently showed him "to be both the most admired and the most despised political figure in Serbia, with results at either extreme

---

[10]Michael Dobbs, "Despairing Serbs Struggle for Survival," *Washington Post*, reprinted in *Manchester Guardian Weekly*, June 27, 1999, p. 15.

[11]See Obrad Kesic, "Serbian Roulette," *Current History*, March 1998, pp. 98–101.

[12]Gordy, March 2000, p. 99.

[13]For a discussion of Milosevic's electoral base, see Gordy, March 2000, pp. 99–102; Eric D. Gordy, *The Culture of Power in Serbia*, University Park, PA: Pennsylvania State University Press, 1999, pp. 19–60, and Robert Thomas, *The Politics of Serbia in the 1990s*, New York: Columbia University Press, 1999, pp. 69–79.

fluctuating between 20 and 25 percent."[14] With such a minimal base of support, Milosevic greatly benefited from the absence of an effective, unified opposition in the FRY.

Milosevic's continued hold on power also stemmed from his ability to manipulate events—particularly nationalist confrontations—to his own ends. Indeed, behind every conflict Milosevic had masterminded, there has "been a parallel struggle against his opponents in Serbia itself":

> [Milosevic] was a politician who had been shaped by the events he appeared to master. There was no hard center to his rule; no strategy. He lived from day to day. The only discernible pattern was perpetual mayhem. Like a high priest of chaos, he caused mischief to exploit for his own purposes. Oblivious to misery and suffering, he promoted conflicts—in Slovenia, in Croatia, in Bosnia, in Serbia itself—to enlarge his power and to keep his own people distracted.[15]

During the 1997 elections, Milosevic's political supporters made heavy and effective use of the Kosovo issue in their election campaigns.[16] To rally popular support in his growing diplomatic confrontations over Kosovo, Milosevic repeatedly played the nationalist card during 1998—most conspicuously in April of that year, when he organized a "referendum on whether there should be international involvement in the Kosovo issue." The vote, which was preceded by a major government media blitz opposing any foreign involvement, was an overwhelming "no" (95 percent against on a 75 percent turnout), which served to further entrench Milosevic's hard-line position on the Kosovo issue.[17]

---

[14]Gordy, March 2000, p. 99.

[15]Doder and Branson, 1999, p. 237.

[16]See Kesic, March 1998, p. 100.

[17]See Memorandum by the Foreign and Commonwealth Office, May 23, 2000.

SOME RAMBOUILLET TERMS WOULD HAVE BEEN UNACCEPTABLE TO THE SERB PUBLIC

Given his long public commitment to the defense of Serb sovereignty and hegemony in Kosovo, Milosevic undoubtedly realized that he would run a serious risk of a massive popular backlash if he were to backpedal on this issue. This was probably the principal reason Milosevic never seriously attempted to negotiate a comprehensive settlement at Rambouillet. While the FRY/Serb delegates at Rambouillet did negotiate about the political arrangement proposed in the agreement, they refused to participate in talks about the security arrangements.[18] Throughout the meetings leading up to the drafting of a final text at Rambouillet, the FRY/Serb delegates frequently played a game of delay and obstruction and sometimes abstained entirely from any constructive participation in the negotiating process.[19] For a time, they apparently hoped that the Kosovo Albanian delegates would refuse to sign the agreement, which would have obviated Belgrade's need to sign as well.

When at the end of the Rambouillet meetings a majority of the Kosovo Albanian delegation voted to accept the text of the agreement, the FRY/Serb delegation demurred but offered to participate in a further round of negotiations. At the Paris follow-on talks, however, the FRY/Serb delegates sought to undo virtually the entire package of agreements negotiated at Rambouillet.[20] The Kosovo Albanian delegation signed the Rambouillet Agreement on March 18, but the FRY/Serb delegates refused, dismissing the Rambouillet text as a "non-agreement" and a Western diktat.[21]

---

[18]See Madeleine K. Albright (secretary of state), press conference following meetings on Kosovo, Rambouillet, France, February 23, 1999, as released by the Office of the Spokesman, Paris, France, U.S. Department of State, http://www.secretary.state.gov/statement/1999/990223.html.

[19]See Marc Weller, "The Rambouillet Conference on Kosovo," *International Affairs*, Vol. 75, No. 2, April 1999, pp. 228–236. For another account of the Rambouillet deliberations, see Ivo H. Daalder and Michael E. O'Hanlon, *Winning Ugly: NATO's War to Save Kosovo*, Washington, D.C.: Brookings Institution Press, 2000, pp. 77–91.

[20]See Memorandum by the Foreign and Commonwealth Office, May 23, 2000.

[21]See Address by Ratko Markovic, Serbian Deputy Prime Minister and head of the Serbian delegation at the Rambouillet and Paris negotiations on Kosovo, in the Serbian parliament on March 23, 1999, as reported on Belgrade Radio, March 23, 1999, *FBIS* translated text, FTS19990323001225.

The Rambouillet provisions that Milosevic and other Serbs found most objectionable were the terms relating to the implementation of the agreement and the mechanism for a final settlement for Kosovo. The Kosovo Albanian delegates, before agreeing to the terms requiring a cease-fire and the disarmament of their forces, demanded that the Rambouillet text also include provisions "for a binding referendum on independence after a three-year interim period, and for a NATO ground force in the meantime. Unsurprisingly, these were also the most difficult points for the Belgrade delegation."[22]

The Kosovo Albanian demand for a NATO ground force was satisfied. The final draft of the agreement empowered NATO to "constitute and lead a military force to help ensure compliance" with the agreement.   In addition, the agreement specified that the implementation force would operate under the authority and be "subject to the direction and the political control of the North Atlantic Council [NAC] through the NATO chain of command."[23] While not so specified in the agreement, the size of this NATO-led force was expected to number around 38,000.

In conjunction with the introduction of this foreign implementation force, the FRY military and police presence in Kosovo was eventually to be reduced to no more than 75 border police and 2500 Yugoslav Army (VJ) border guard and support troops, whose operational area was to be restricted to a 5-km zone along Kosovo's international borders.[24] Taken together, these provisions would have ceded the control of Kosovo to foreign troops, which was a prospect that was anathema both to Milosevic and to most Serbs.

Equally unacceptable to the Serb side was a clause added at the insistence of the Kosovo Albanian delegation that stipulated that

---

[22]Memorandum by the Foreign and Commonwealth Office, May 23, 2000.

[23]The force was to be "composed of ground, air, and maritime units from NATO and non-NATO nations." See Rambouillet Agreement, *Interim Agreement for Peace and Self-Government in Kosovo*, Chapter 7, Implementation II, Article I: General Obligations, 1 (a and b).

[24]See Rambouillet Agreement, Chapter 2, Article VI (2, a), and Chapter 7, Article IV: VJ Forces.

after three years the final status of Kosovo would be determined, *inter alia,* by "the will of the people":

> Three years after the entry into force of this Agreement, an international meeting shall be convened to determine a mechanism for a final settlement for Kosovo, on the basis of the will of the people, opinions of relevant authorities, each Party's efforts regarding the implementation of this Agreement, and the Helsinki Final Act, and to undertake a comprehensive assessment of the implementation of this Agreement and to consider proposals by any Party for additional measures.[25]

While the wording of this provision fell far short of the "binding referendum" the Kosovo Albanians had demanded, their delegation obtained a written assurance (albeit in draft form) from the United States that this formula confirmed "a right for the people of Kosovo to hold a referendum on the final status of Kosovo after three years." The assurance was conveyed in a draft letter that the Kosovo Albanian delegates were told Secretary of State Albright would sign if their delegation signed the Rambouillet Agreement by a set deadline.[26]

Realizing that such a referendum would almost certainly produce a majority vote for independence, Milosevic must have viewed this

---

[25]Rambouillet Agreement, Chapter 8, Amendment, Comprehensive, Assessment, and Final Clauses, Article I: Amendment and Comprehensive Assessment, (3).

[26]The text of the letter read as follows:

Rambouillet, 22 February 1999

This letter concerns the formulation (attached) proposed for Chapter 8, Article I (3) of the interim Framework Agreement. We will regard this proposal, or any other formulation, of that Article that may be agreed at Rambouillet, as confirming a right for the people of Kosovo to hold a referendum on the final status of Kosovo after three years.

Sincerely,
Madeleine Albright, Secretary of State

See Judah, 2000, p. 215. It should be noted that the United States was guaranteeing the Kosovars a referendum no matter how Chapter 8, Article I (3) actually read. Furthermore, as Weller has noted, the assurance established a "legal right to hold a referendum of the people of Kosovo (as opposed, say, to the people of the FRY or the Serb Republic)." See Weller, April 1999, pp. 232 and 245.

provision as tantamount to guaranteeing Kosovo's eventual separation from the FRY. Even if the "will of the people" was only one of the several factors that were to determine a mechanism for a final settlement, it would have been "difficult," as a House of Commons report on the war put it, "to envisage a situation where a referendum would be held and then disregarded by the international community."[27]

A final provision of the Rambouillet Agreement that would have proven unacceptable to FRY/Serb delegates had they been interested in actually negotiating a settlement concerned the status of NATO forces in the FRY. Chapter 7, Appendix B, gave NATO personnel, "together with their vehicles, vessels, aircraft, and equipment, free and unrestricted passage and unimpeded access throughout the FRY including associated air space and territorial waters. This shall include, but not be limited to, the right to bivouac, maneuver, billet, and utilization of any areas or facilities as required for support, training, and operations."[28] Among other rights, it also authorized NATO, as needed in the conduct of its operations, "to make improvements or modifications to certain infrastructure in the FRY, such as roads, bridges, tunnels, buildings, and utility systems."[29]

Needless to say, such sweeping authority to infringe on FRY sovereignty was unacceptable to the FRY/Serb delegates, even if they did not cite it at the time as a principal reason for their refusal to accept the Rambouillet Agreement.[30] However, the Serbs would

---

[27]See "The Kosovo Crisis After May 1997," Select Committee on Foreign Affairs, Fourth Report, House of Commons, May 23, 2000, http://www.parliament. the.stationary.off.../pa/cm/199900/cmselect/cmfaff/28/2808/html.

[28]Rambouillet Agreement, Chapter 7, Appendix B: Status of Multi-National Military Implementation Force, (8).

[29]Rambouillet Agreement, Chapter 7, Appendix B: Status of Multi-National Military Implementation Force, (22).

[30]It is likely the Contact Group negotiators would have agreed to revise Chapter 7, Appendix B, and limit the status-of-forces rights only to the territory of Kosovo had this been necessary to secure the FRY/Serb delegation's signature on the Rambouillet Agreement. Western officials interviewed in the course of this research were unanimous in the view that the members of the Contact Group were ready to show significant flexibility in softening the terms of Chapter 7, Appendix B, of the Rambouillet Agreement. As it was, no changes were made in these terms because the FRY/Serb delegates refused to engage.

later make much of the fact that no such rights were accorded NATO or other foreign forces in the June 1999 war termination agreement.

ACCEPTING RAMBOUILLET WOULD HAVE BEEN DANGEROUS FOR MILOSEVIC

Milosevic probably calculated that accepting Rambouillet's terms without a fight or a consensus to yield on them among the Serbian populace would have endangered his continued hold on power. Milosevic had, after all, promised that Kosovo would "forever" be firmly tied to Serbia and that he would force the Kosovo Albanians to respect the Serbian authorities. Should he now accept the almost complete withdrawal of Serb army and police forces from Kosovo and the deployment of NATO troops in the province, he would undermine the foundation on which he had built his political career.[31]

Furthermore, it was clear that a large majority of the Serbian public opposed allowing foreign troops to enter Kosovo. Surveys conducted in February and March 1999 showed that the number of Serbian respondents opposing NATO troops in Kosovo had grown from about 78 percent at the time of the Rambouillet talks to more than 91 percent by the time of the final Paris meeting.[32] No less than 69 percent of the respondents in a March telephone poll conducted by the Belgrade weekly *Nin* expressed the belief that Kosovo should be defended "at any cost" and said they stood ready to take part in its defense.[33]

Milosevic almost certainly knew that a majority of the population would identify the arrival of foreign troops in Kosovo as "aggression." The instant Kosovo was no longer under Serbian military and police control, the Serbian voters would consider the province to be "lost" and "surrendered" to Albanian governance. As a consequence,

---

[31]See "The Kosovo Talks: Holbrooke as Last Chance," BETA, March 11, 1999, BETA Commentary, *FBIS* translated text, FTS19990311000225.

[32]See *V.I.P. Daily News Report 1467*, March 23, 1999, p. 5.

[33]The telephone opinion poll was based on a sample of 200 randomly selected Serbian citizens. See "Opinion Poll: 78.5% of Citizens Do Not Expect Air Strikes," BETA, March 18, 1999, *FBIS* translated excerpt, FTS19990318001456.

Milosevic would face tremendous voter opposition in the new elections that would become unavoidable if the Rambouillet Agreement were fully implemented.[34] Milosevic also knew that a decision to accept foreign troops would strengthen the influence and electoral prospects of the ultranationalist Serbian Radical Party, which would strongly oppose such a concession.[35]

Milosevic was apparently being told by some of his VJ and other senior advisers that he would be "better off with NATO air strikes than with NATO ground troops in Kosovo." Indeed, those hawkish advisers apparently asserted that the rally-around-the-flag effects of air strikes would serve to strengthen Milosevic's political hand and that his position in Yugoslavia would "wax stronger with each new bomb dropped."[36]

Other advisers were reportedly counseling another course of action, cautioning that bombing "could prove dangerous" for the regime, but their advice was not being heeded. In the end, Milosevic came down on the side of rejecting Rambouillet. His decision to do so apparently reflected the judgment that he could be ousted from office if NATO troops entered Kosovo but that "air strikes would not bring about his overthrow."[37]

The calculations of some allied leaders that Milosevic would come to heel and accept the terms of the Rambouillet Agreement after a few days of bombing seem to have been predicated on a misestimate of how Milosevic would view his options. Their miscalculations seem to have been influenced at least in part by the effectiveness of limited NATO bombing in bringing the conflict in Bosnia-Herzegovina to a close in 1995 and by the Dayton negotiation experience, where

---

[34]The elections in Kosovo to select new delegates for the Serbian legislature and the FRY parliament mandated by the Rambouillet Agreement would almost certainly have required new elections in Serbia and Montenegro as well. See "BETA Examines Milosevic's Kosovo Options, BETA, March 4, 1999, *FBIS* translated text, FTS19990304000223, and "BETA Sees Belgrade Profiting from Strikes," BETA, March 18, 1999, *FBIS* translated text, FTS19990318000546.

[35]See "The Kosovo Talks: Holbrooke as Last Chance," March 11, 1999.

[36]See *V.I.P. Daily News Report 1465,* March 19, 1999, p. 2, and *1471*, March 27, 1999, p. 4.

[37]See *V.I.P. Daily News Report 1465,* March 19, 1999, p. 2, and *1471*, March 27, 1999, p. 4.

Milosevic conceded on most of the demands being made of the Bosnian Serbs. The NATO leaders may also have been misled by Milosevic's apparent readiness to yield under a NATO bombing threat in October 1998. But this time the stakes were different, for as the authors of one study put it, Milosevic "could not relinquish Kosovo—which Serbs regarded as the heart of Serbia itself—and hope to survive."[38]

---

[38]See Doder and Branson, 1999, p. 8.

Chapter Three

HE ASSUMED HE COULD FORCE NATO TO OFFER BETTER TERMS

Once the bombing started, many NATO officials were unpleasantly surprised by Milosevic's stubborn refusal to concede. The reason Milosevic did not yield early on was that he believed he could (1) absorb the costs of the expected bombing, and (2) eventually secure terms more favorable to Serbia than those proposed in the Rambouillet Agreement.

MILOSEVIC HAD REASON TO EXPECT THE BOMBING TO BE LIMITED

While Milosevic apparently expected to be bombed, his intelligence sources and perceptions of recent U.S. and NATO behavior may have encouraged him to believe that any NATO air strikes would be of limited duration and severity.

Perhaps because the warnings NATO had voiced earlier in 1998 about possible military action had come to naught, Milosevic, in October 1998, initially evidenced some skepticism that NATO would resort to bombing over Kosovo. At one point during his negotiations with Richard Holbrooke, Milosevic asked, "Are you crazy enough to bomb us over these issues we're talking about in that lousy little Kosovo?" Holbrooke responded, "You bet, we're just crazy enough to do it."[1] In the course of those meetings, Holbrooke and the

---

[1]See Interview with Richard Holbrooke, PBS *Frontline*, "War in Europe," February 22, 2000, http://www.pbs.org/wgbh/pages/frontline/shows/kosovo/interviews.

AIRSOUTH commander, Lieutenant General Michael Short, made a concerted effort to persuade Milosevic and his military leaders that the threat of bombing was real.[2] Holbrooke attributes Milosevic's eventual agreement in October 1998 to accept unarmed OSCE monitors and reduce Serb forces in Kosovo partly to the credibility of NATO's threat to bomb.[3]

The evidence suggests that Milosevic fully expected NATO bombing if he refused to sign the Rambouillet Agreement. The fact that the Serbs had moved their forces out of their garrisons, dispersed petroleum, oil, and lubricant (POL) stocks, and evacuated a number of likely targets prior to March 24 suggests that Milosevic attached considerable credibility to the warnings he had received from various NATO leaders and special envoys about the consequences that would flow from a rejection of Rambouillet. One of the last of these warnings was delivered on March 21, when Holbrooke and his team presented the ultimatum to Milosevic that if he didn't sign the Rambouillet Agreement, "the bombing would start." Holbrooke met privately with the Yugoslav leader to make certain he understood what would follow his refusal:

> I said to him, "You understand that if I leave here without an agreement today, bombing will start almost immediately." And he said, "Yes, I understand that." I said, "You understand it'll be swift, severe, and sustained." And I used those three words very carefully, after consultations with the Pentagon. And he said, "You're a great country, a powerful country. You can do anything you want. We can't stop you." . . . I said, "Yes, you understand. You're absolutely clear what will happen when we leave?" And he said, very quietly, "Yes. You'll bomb us."[4]

---

[2]When General Short joined Holbrooke in the middle of the negotiations, Milosevic's opening remark was, "So, General, you're the man who's gonna bomb us?" General Short responded with a line he and Holbrooke had rehearsed on the plane flying into Belgrade: "Mr. President, I have B52s in one hand, and I have U2s in the other. It's up to you which one I'm going to have to use." See Interview with Richard Holbrooke, February 22, 2000.

[3]According to Holbrooke, the other factors prompting Milosevic to agree were the unified position of the Contact Group and Russia's willingness to go along with the arrangements being proposed. See Interview with Richard Holbrooke, February 22, 2000.

[4]See Interview with Richard Holbrooke, February 22, 2000.

While Milosevic was convinced the FRY would be bombed, it is less clear that he believed the bombing would be "severe and sustained" as Holbrooke had warned. Indeed, it is likely that Milosevic was receiving information from other sources that indicated the NATO bombing would be short-lived and "manageable" in terms of the destruction it would bring—for the reports that pervaded NATO circles about a brief two- to three-day bombing campaign were also circulating in Belgrade. A journalist with *Vreme* magazine in Belgrade reported that two different Western sources told him that the initial strikes would last only three days "to give Milosevic something to think about." He was further told that if Milosevic still remained defiant, additional strikes would follow and continue until Milosevic came to terms or was replaced by "someone more sensitive to Western demands."[5]

Milosevic may have had inside diplomatic information on NATO's intentions. Holbrooke sensed that Milosevic had received intelligence from one of the NATO countries or the Russians to the effect that the bombing would be "light."[6] A French intelligence officer, Major Pierre-Henri Bunel, who held a senior post at NATO headquarters in Brussels, has admitted passing "harmless" details of NATO bombing targets to Serbian intelligence agents.[7] In sum, Milosevic and the other Yugoslav leaders seem to have had advanced information about the likely scope, the predicted duration, and apparently even the targets of the initial NATO attacks.

A brief bombing campaign may also have appeared credible to Milosevic because of the precedent set by the December 1998 Operation Desert Fox air campaign, in which U.S. and UK forces attacked Iraq for its refusal to permit U.N. inspections of suspected weapons of mass destruction (WMD) sites. The operative lesson for

---

[5]See Dejan Anastasijevic, "Apres Slobo, the Deluge," *Institute for War and Peace Reporting*, March 24, 1999, http://iwpr.vs4.ccrbernet.co.uk/index.pl?archive/bcr/bcr_19990324_1_eng.txt.

[6]Judah, 2000, p. 229.

[7]Bunel claimed that he was "trying to win credibility" so as to convince Serbia that the NATO allies were committed to an attack if Serbia did not come to terms on Kosovo and that the senior French officer at NATO was aware of his contacts with Serbian intelligence. See Charles Bremmer, "NATO 'Spy' Says France Used Him," *London Times*, June 9, 2000.

Milosevic was that even though Saddam refused to yield, the bombing was terminated after four days. In this respect, Milosevic may have expected that any NATO bombing would be more akin to Operation Desert Fox than to Operation Desert Storm.

MILOSEVIC BELIEVED HE COULD FORCE A HALT TO THE BOMBING AND GARNER BETTER TERMS

Even if the bombing proved more severe and sustained than expected, however, Milosevic seems to have assumed that he had the means to eventually create sufficient countervailing pressures on the NATO allies to cause them to terminate the bombing and agree to interim arrangements for Kosovo that were more acceptable to Belgrade. In particular, Milosevic apparently calculated that NATO's unity could be undermined.

Milosevic's and NATO's Terms Were Diametrically Opposed

In Milosevic's thinking, the only terms that would have been acceptable were those that would have left Serbia in de facto control of Kosovo no matter what the degree of putative autonomy Belgrade might have to promise the Kosovo Albanians. As of late April 1999, Milosevic was still demanding a settlement that would:

- Ensure the FRY's continued territorial integrity and sovereignty over Kosovo. This meant, among other things, that the agreement must exclude any provision for a referendum or other arrangement that might lead to Kosovo's independence.[8]

- Permit a significant FRY military and police presence to remain in Kosovo. Milosevic was willing to reduce VJ forces in Kosovo only to "the normal garrison strength of between 11,000 and 12,000, which was the regular Pristina Corps."[9]

---

[8]It should be noted that the United States and most (if not all) other NATO allies also opposed independence for Kosovo.

[9]See Arnaud de Borchgrave, "We Are Willing to Defend Our Rights," *Washington Times*, May 1, 1999, p. 8, for his interview with Milosevic on April 29, 1999.

- Restrict the weaponry, composition, and functions of any foreign peacekeeping mission in Kosovo. The peacekeepers were to carry "defensive arms" only, could not include troops from the NATO combatants, and could act only as "observers" to monitor the peace.[10]

- Make the United Nations the controlling body of any foreign security and civil presence in the province. Milosevic saw obvious advantages to having any foreign civil or security presence in Kosovo under the ultimate command and control of the U.N. Security Council, where Russia and China could wield the veto.[11]

To deprive NATO of its bargaining leverage, Milosevic wanted a "cessation of all military activities" (a halt to the bombing) prior to the negotiation of any political settlement. Again to weaken NATO's leverage, he also demanded that any decrease of VJ troops in Kosovo be matched by a withdrawal of NATO troops away from Kosovo's borders with Albania and Macedonia.[12] Finally, as the subsequent discussion will show, Milosevic undoubtedly also wanted to control and limit the return of the refugees who had been expelled from Kosovo.

In virtually every respect except the matter of independence for Kosovo, Milosevic's terms for a settlement were diametrically opposed to the conditions that NATO had laid down for war termination. These terms, which were to remain valid throughout the conflict, were first enunciated on April 6, 1999, and called on Milosevic to:

- ensure a verifiable cessation of all combat activities and killings

- withdraw his military, police, and paramilitary forces from Kosovo

---

[10]See de Borchgrave, May 1, 1999, p. 8. Milosevic was still adhering to many of these demands when he met with Chernomyrdin on May 27. See also Chapter Eight.

[11]Milosevic's preference for the United Nations as the controlling body no doubt also stemmed from the fact that the Serbs had had considerable success in constraining and manipulating U.N.-commanded peacekeeping forces in Bosnia-Herzegovina.

[12]See de Borchgrave, May 1, 1999, p. 8.

- agree to the deployment of an international security force in Kosovo[13]
- permit the unconditional return of all refugees and unimpeded access for humanitarian aid
- join in putting in place a political framework for Kosovo on the basis of the Rambouillet accords.[14]

NATO also insisted that the bombing be halted only after the negotiations had been completed and the FRY had agreed to the above conditions. In essence, NATO was insisting that Milosevic agree to the terms he had rejected at Rambouillet with the added fillip that he permit the unconditional return of all refugees.

Milosevic Assumed He Could Undermine NATO's Unity and Resolve

When Chernomyrdin first met with Milosevic on April 22, the FRY leader exuded confidence:

> He was calm and purposeful. He was confident in that he was right, he would win, and NATO would lose and his nation was supporting him, which was true at the time. There was no opposition. Everybody was in harmony.[15]

A key reason for this confidence was Milosevic's belief that the NATO governments would not remain steadfast in their support of the bombing and that they could eventually be persuaded to accept terms close to those being offered by Belgrade. He was no doubt encouraged in this view by the irresolution NATO had displayed in past dealings with the FRY over Kosovo and the apparent differences of opinion that existed among the allies about the use of force.

---

[13]NATO later specified that the international force be under NATO command and control and include "substantial" NATO participation.

[14]Press statement by James P. Rubin, spokesman, U.S. Department of State, Office of the Spokesman, April 6, 1999. A similar set of conditions were issued by the heads of state and government participating in the meeting of the NAC in Washington, D.C., on April 23–24, 1999. See NATO Press Release S-1(99)62, April 23, 1999.

[15]See Interview with Viktor Chernomyrdin, PBS *Frontline*, "War in Europe," February 22, 2000, http://www.pbs.org/wgbh/pages/frontline/shows/kosovo/interviews.

Furthermore, it seemed clear that Milosevic assumed that the FRY could promote the erosion of NATO unity and resolve by (1) engaging in ethnic cleansing, (2) undermining support for the war among NATO and other foreign publics, and (3) exploiting Russia's support for the FRY.

Assumed Ethnic Cleansing Would Provide Leverage. There can be little doubt that Belgrade planned and controlled at least the broad dimensions of the massive ethnic cleansing campaign that VJ and MUP forces conducted against the Kosovo Albanian population during the first half of 1999. The OSCE's in-depth investigation of human rights violations in Kosovo revealed that there was an "overall approach" to the cleansing that "appeared highly organized and systematic. Everywhere, the attacks on communities appear to have been dictated by strategy, not by breakdown in command and control."[16] Between March and June of 1999, no fewer than 863,000 Kosovo Albanians were expelled from Kosovo, of whom some 440,000 remained in Albania and some 248,000 in Macedonia (see Figure 3.1).[17] In addition, perhaps as many as 590,000 other Kosovo Albanians were displaced within Kosovo and remained in the province throughout the conflict.[18] All told, the OSCE estimates that more than 90 percent of the Kosovo Albanian population may have been displaced in 1999.[19]

Milosevic and the other Serb leaders apparently calculated that this massive campaign of ethnic cleansing would both help solidify

---

[16]For the OSCE's comprehensive report on human rights violations in Kosovo during the period October 1998 to June 1999, see OSCE, *Kosovo, As Seen, As Told,* December 1999, http://www.osce.org/kosovo/reports.html. The report was based on an analysis of the OSCE Kosovo Verification Mission's human rights files compiled in Kosovo up to the mission's withdrawal on March 20, 1999, and on some 2800 victim and direct witness statements taken by OSCE human rights officers in the refugee camps of Macedonia and Albania during the air campaign.

[17]Some 70,000 Kosovo Albanian refugees also fled to Montenegro and some 22,000 to Bosnia-Herzegovina. An additional 80,000 refugees were evacuated to some 40 other countries. See OSCE, December 1999, Part I, Chapter 14, pp. 1–3.

[18]The United Nations High Commissioner for Refugees estimated an internally displaced population of 590,000 as of May 13, 1999. However, the absence of international observers on the ground in Kosovo made it impossible to verify this estimate.

[19]OSCE, December 1999, Part I, Chapter 14, p. 1.

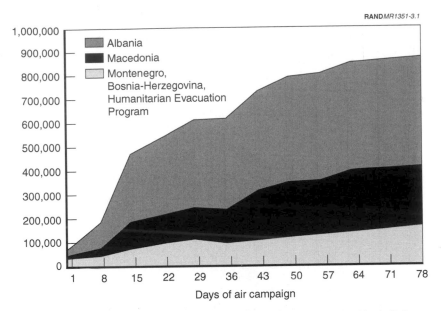

SOURCE: OSCE, *Kosovo, As Seen, As Told*, Part I, Chapter 14, pp. 2–3.

Figure 3.1—Flow of Refugees from Kosovo, March 23–June 9, 1999

Belgrade's hold on Kosovo and improve its bargaining leverage with NATO. Based on the pattern of the cleansing and the Serb statements that accompanied it, we can infer that the ethnic cleansing was probably intended to serve several objectives simultaneously— namely, to (1) eliminate the KLA as a factor in any future settlement, (2) show NATO that its bombing was counterproductive and confront the Alliance with acute humanitarian crises in Albania and Macedonia, and (3) permanently reduce the size of the Kosovo Albanian majority in Kosovo.

Eliminate the KLA as a factor in any future settlement. Milosevic apparently assumed that he could effectively halt KLA attacks on the Kosovo Serbs and eliminate the KLA as a major factor in any future settlement by systematically destroying the KLA forces and support bases within Kosovo. He further believed that the insurgents and their supporters could be crushed with relative ease once the inspection regimes and other constraints that had been imposed on Serbia by the October 1998 agreements were lifted. Indeed, he boasted to General Clark that his forces would "just need seven days to wipe out" the KLA![20]

The Serbian style of counterinsurgency operations was ethnic cleansing, and instances of ethnic cleansing—sometimes in response to KLA provocations—continued to occur in Kosovo during the early weeks of 1999. However, anti-KLA ethnic cleansing dramatically escalated after the OSCE verifiers were withdrawn from Kosovo on March 20. The VJ and MUP forces initially concentrated on securing Kosovo's key lines of communication (LOCs), moving Kosovo Albanians out of villages lying along strategic routes and at important crossroads. Shortly thereafter, the Serbian security forces began cleansing other areas of known KLA operations. Kosovo Albanian men of fighting age were routinely separated from women and children during ethnic cleansing operations and sometimes executed.[21] Serb forces also took up positions along Kosovo's borders with Albania and Macedonia to prevent the reinfiltration of KLA forces into the province.

Show the bombing to be counterproductive by creating a humanitarian crisis. An apparent second purpose of the ethnic cleansing was to bring pressure on NATO by creating acute humanitarian crises in Kosovo and in neighboring Macedonia and Albania.[22] Milosevic and his colleagues apparently believed that generating massive numbers of internal and external refugees would create negotiating leverage for Belgrade by:

---

[20]Roger Cohen, "Milosevic's Vision of Glory Unleashed Decades of Ruin," *New York Times*, July 2, 1999, pp. A1 and A8.

[21]OSCE, December 1999, Part I, Chapter 3, pp. 8–9.

[22]An independent Belgrade news service with sources inside the regime predicted on March 26, 1999, that

> Milosevic will try to destabilize the entire southern Balkans and expand the conflict to Macedonia, Bosnia, and Albania to scare his adversaries in NATO. He intends to expel a large number of Albanians from Kosovo in order to provoke a reaction from Western Europe, which already does not know what to do with masses of Albanian refugees and fake asylum seekers.

See *V.I.P. Daily News Report 1471*, March 27, 1999, p. 4.

- Demonstrating that the bombing was counterproductive in that it was creating and sustaining a humanitarian crisis rather than preventing one, as had been promised by the NATO leaders. Milosevic claimed that the refugee flight was the product of NATO's air attacks and that the bombing must be halted if the refugees were to return home.[23]

- Confronting the NATO governments with the possibility that their countries might be called on to absorb additional large numbers of Balkan refugees, something the Western European governments were loath to do. As of March 23, 1999, there were already "more than one million refugees" from the former Yugoslavia in the European Union (EU) countries.[24]

- Threatening NATO with the destabilization of Macedonia and the reignition of unrest in Albania.[25] Both countries lacked the economic resources, transportation infrastructure, food supplies, and administrative experience to cope with a massive influx of refugees. The tide of Kosovo refugees flowing into Macedonia posed a potentially explosive political problem for that ethnically divided country.[26] The message Milosevic sought to convey was that the NATO bombing, rather than containing Balkan unrest, was promoting it.

There can be little question that the massive expulsion of Kosovo Albanians was a planned riposte to the NATO bombing. As soon as

---

[23]In his April 29 interview with Arnaud de Borchgrave, Milosevic stated that the first task of the "temporary joint executive board for Kosovo" he was thinking of forming was going to be to help the "refugees return home." However, Milosevic told de Borchgrave that "the problem for returning [the] refugees will be [the] bombing. So clearly this insanity will have to stop. Before [the] bombing, regardless of what you hear from NATO and Pentagon briefings, there were no refugees. It wasn't only the Albanians who fled, but also the Serbs, Turks, everyone." See de Borchgrave, May 1, 1999, p. 8.

[24]See Statement of Prime Minister Tony Blair before the House of Commons, March 23, 1999, quoted in *Kosovo: The Military Campaign*, Select Committee on Foreign Affairs, Fourth Report, House of Commons, May 23, 2000, http://www.parliament.the.stationary.off.../pa/cm/199900/cmselect/cmfaff/28/2812.html.

[25]Ibid.

[26]For a discussion of the threat posed by the refugee to Macedonian stability, see Duncan Perry, "Macedonia's Quest for Security and Stability," *Current History*, March 2000, pp. 129–136.

the bombing began on March 24, the ethnic cleansing rapidly expanded into non-KLA areas and eventually encompassed villages and municipalities throughout the province. From March 24 to the morning of April 2—a space of a little more than a week—a total of 177,500 Kosovo Albanians arrived in Macedonia, Albania, and nearby countries. On April 3 alone, an additional 130,000 refugees arrived in Macedonia and Albania. According to the OSCE,

> The arrival of such large numbers so soon after the departure of the OSCE-KVM [Kosovo Verification Mission] would appear to indicate pre-planning of the operations. After this first influx, the routes which internally displaced persons (IDPs) took within Kosovo were regulated by Serbian forces. The flow of refugees was also regulated, with the result that many thousands would arrive at border crossing points . . . on some days, but then only a handful of refugees would arrive at particular crossing points on succeeding days. Such patterns provide a further indication that the operation was clearly planned and executed, not least with a view to keeping key communication routes within Kosovo open.[27]

Permanently reduce the size of the Kosovo Albanian majority. Milosevic may also have assumed that the campaign of systematic ethnic cleansing would result in a permanent change in Kosovo's ethnic balance. Diluting the Kosovo Albanian majority in Kosovo had been a long-held goal of the extreme Serbian nationalists, and Milosevic may have calculated that he could confront NATO with a *fait accompli* that would stand up in a future cease-fire or settlement. Ethnic cleansing had been the dominant modus operandi of the forces contesting for control of Bosnia-Herzegovina, and the experience of the various combatants in that conflict was that once refugees were expelled from an area, they rarely returned.[28]

While Milosevic and other senior Serb leaders adamantly denied that Serbia was seeking to change Kosovo's ethnic balance and pledged to allow the safe return of refugees once the bombing stopped, other Serb officials privately admitted that a permanent reduction of the

---

[27]OSCE, December 1999, Part I, Chapter 14, p. 2.

[28]American and other peacekeeping forces in Bosnia-Herzegovina had tacitly accepted the results of ethnic cleansing because they were loath to attempt to reintegrate and thereafter defend formerly displaced populations by force of arms.

Kosovo Albanian population was the aim. Serb officials in Kosovo reportedly told a senior European diplomat that they were trying to curtail Kosovo Albanian power by remaking the province's demographic balance. The officials said they had already reduced the number of Kosovo Albanians to "a roughly tolerable level" and hoped to have only about 600,000 Kosovo Albanians living in Kosovo when the war was over. One reason they offered for retaining a sizable number of Kosovo Albanians in the province was to help protect the Serbs against a NATO ground attack.[29]

The pattern of ethnic cleansing supports the thesis that the Serbs sought to prevent the return of externally displaced refugees. The refugees' houses were burned to dissuade them from returning, and their documents were routinely confiscated by Serbian authorities, often while the refugees were en route to or at the borders before crossing into Albania and Macedonia.[30]

The confiscation of documents was ominous in that the Serbian position at least through late April 1999 was that only persons who could prove that they were citizens of Kosovo were going to be allowed to return.[31] Since Serbian officials regularly claimed that some 300,000 Kosovo Albanians who had entered Kosovo from Albania during the past decade were never Yugoslav citizens, it seems likely that the Serbs intended to deny reentry to many, if not all, undocumented refugees had Serb authorities remained in control of Kosovo's borders.[32]

Assumed Human Costs of Bombing Would Erode Public Support for the War. Chernomyrdin reports that Milosevic held to a hard line on Kosovo at the beginning of their negotiations on April 22 because he "still hoped that the international public would rebel against the

---

[29]See Steven Erlanger, "Diplomat Says Serbs Want Some Albanians in Kosovo," *New York Times*, April 25, 1999, p. 14.

[30]According to the OSCE report, some refugees left their documents in their houses because they had to leave so suddenly or had had them confiscated at a police station or in prison. Tractor and car license plates and documents were also taken. OSCE, December 1999, Part I, Chapter 14, p. 18.

[31]As Goran Matic, a Serbian cabinet minister, put it: "We would like all the Albanians to come back, all those who can prove they were citizens of Yugoslavia." Erlanger, April 25, 1999, p. 14.

[32]Erlanger, April 25, 1999, p. 14.

[NATO] aggression."[33] This hope was undoubtedly based in large part on the expectation that the civilian Serb casualties incurred during the bombing would turn the NATO publics against the war and cause them to bring pressure on their governments to halt the bombing. Sources close to the Belgrade regime reported in late March that Milosevic "believed he could tolerate NATO air strikes long enough to generate serious political changes in Russia and Western Europe, which would enable him to come out of the war with NATO and the United States a political winner."[34]

Public statements such as the April 28 address by the head of the FRY's Supreme Command Headquarters, Lieutenant General Dragoljub Ojdanic, provide insights on how the Belgrade leaders hoped the international public would react to the bombing:

> News about our heroic resistance in spite of the obstacles and fabrications launched by the new fascist propaganda are gradually reaching the world. Every day a growing number of people throughout Europe and the world over are raising their voice in protest against the insane crimes of the aggressors, realizing that peace and the future of Mankind is threatened.[35]

Postwar interviews with senior Serb officials, including some of Milosevic's "closest friends and advisers," disclosed that the Belgrade leaders expected the mounting civilian casualties from the bombing to cause a major rift between NATO governments within a matter of weeks. In particular, the Serb leaders expected France to break ranks with the United States once civilian casualties began to grow.[36]

---

[33]Alberto Stabile, interview with Viktor Chernomyrdin, June 10, 1999, as reported in *Rome La Republica*, June 11, 1999, *FBIS* translated text, FTS19990611000441.

[34]See *V.I.P. Daily News Report 1471*, March 27, 1999, p. 4.

[35]See Yugoslav Army Supreme Command Headquarters—Information Service, Daily Review 26, "Statement by the Head of the Supreme Command HQ, Lieutenant General Dragoljub Ojdanic," Press Center, April 28, 1999.

[36]The officials were interviewed by Arnaud de Borchgrave shortly after the settlement was reached. According to de Borchgrave, none of the officials "would speak on the record. But privately, they had no compunction about unburdening themselves." See Arnaud de Borchgrave, "Serbs Concede Making Big Miscalculation," *Washington Times*, June 11, 1999, p. 1.

To generate public opposition to the bombing, the Belgrade regime orchestrated a sustained information campaign about the civilian casualties and collateral damage the bombing had caused. Foreign newspersons, who otherwise were typically confined to Belgrade, were provided access to sites of errant bombing throughout the countryside. Incidents of civilian casualties and collateral damage were the primary subject matter of the Belgrade government's foreign and domestic television broadcasts, Internet Web sites, and daily press handouts.

During the course of the air campaign, Belgrade also surfaced a number of "peace proposals" designed to generate international support for a bombing halt and a "compromise" solution to the Kosovo problem. These peace initiatives included the announcement of unilateral cease-fires and troop withdrawals; publicized negotiations with Rugova, the titular head of the former Kosovo Albanian government; the release of the three American GIs who had wandered into Serbian territory; and various proposals concerning the establishment of a lightly armed peacekeeping presence in Kosovo under U.N. command and control.

Finally, Milosevic undoubtedly also hoped to gain bargaining leverage with NATO by downing NATO aircraft and killing or capturing NATO airmen.[37] Like other enemy leaders who have proved willing to confront more powerful Western forces, Milosevic apparently saw the allies' reluctance to absorb casualties as their Achilles' heel. He told one U.S. interviewer that the NATO allies had miscalculated in attacking Serbia because "you are not willing to sacrifice lives to achieve our surrender."[38]

Assumed He Could Exploit Russia's Support for the FRY. Milosevic and other senior Serb officials clearly assumed that Serbia would receive sustained support from Russia in its confrontation with

---

[37]According to one account, Milosevic's military chiefs had promised him that with their existing air defense systems they could, within a relatively short time, shoot down 10 to 20 NATO aircraft. See Judah, 2000, p. 232.

[38]Milosevic also asserted that "the U.S. Congress is beginning to understand that bombing a country into compliance is not a viable policy or strategy." See de Borchgrave, May 1, 1999, p. 8.

NATO.[39] The Serbs were encouraged in this belief by the unwavering backing the Russians had given the Yugoslav delegation despite its obstructionist tactics during the Rambouillet and Paris talks; the expressions of support some Russian leaders had given Milosevic during their visits to Belgrade; and the adamant opposition Moscow had voiced to any bombing.[40] Milosevic and his advisers counted on the fact that once hostilities began, Serbia would receive the sympathetic backing of Russia's military leaders, the Russian Duma, and Russian public opinion.

The Serbs were reinforced in this belief by the wave of anti-American sentiment and support for Serbia that swept through Russia following the start of the NATO bombing. Reflecting this upsurge in popular feeling, the communist-led Duma, by a vote of 279 to 30, demanded on April 7 that the government send military aid and advisers to Yugoslavia—an action that would have violated the U.N. sanctions prohibiting arms aid to Belgrade.[41]

It is possible that Belgrade hoped not only for arms transfers but for even more direct aid.[42] Chernomyrdin reports that Milosevic "tried very hard" to get Russia to join in the conflict. In one attempt to involve Russia more deeply, Milosevic proposed that the FRY formerly join in a union with Belarus and Russia.[43]

---

[39]See de Borchgrave, June 11, 1999, p. 1.

[40]Oleg Levitin, a former Russian foreign ministry official who was directly involved in Moscow's Balkan policies during 1990–1999, has suggested that Moscow's "stubbornness" in supporting the Yugoslav negotiators at Rambouillet and Paris "gave a false signal to Belgrade and contributed to its tougher stand." See Oleg Levitin, "Inside Moscow's Kosovo Muddle," *Survival,* Spring 2000, p. 137.

[41]Celestine Bohlen, "'Don't Push Us,' Yeltsin Warns West on Balkans," *New York Times,* April 10, 1999, p. A8.

[42]When asked by Russian state TV RTR on March 16, 1999, whether the FRY would request Russia's military assistance if it came under attack, Borislav Milosevic, Belgrade's ambassador to Russia and Milosevic's brother, stated that he could not rule out that Yugoslavia might, in such a case, be forced to request military assistance from "friendly countries."

[43]Reacting to Milosevic's proposal for a union with Belarus and Russia, Chernomyrdin reports asking the Serbian leader: "Where have you been before? Why didn't you put forward [this proposal] before the war? Union is good, we can set [it] up. But first, what we need now is to stop the war which is going on between NATO and Yugoslavia." See Interview with Viktor Chernomyrdin, PBS *Frontline,* "War in Europe," February 22, 2000.

Boris Yeltsin was also convinced that Milosevic was hoping for more direct Russian involvement. According to Yeltsin,

> Milosevic behaved utterly without principle. In his relations with Russia, he . . . wagered on an explosion of popular dissatisfaction with my foreign policy. He anticipated a split in Russian society and hoped to push Russia into a political and military confrontation with the West.[44]

At a minimum, Milosevic expected Russia to put political pressure on NATO to stop the bombing and to support the FRY diplomatically. In this respect, he calculated that Russia's involvement in the negotiations with NATO would protect Belgrade's interests.

---

[44]Boris Yeltsin, *Midnight Diaries*, translated by Catherine A. Fitzpatrick, New York: Public Affairs, 2000, p. 265.

Part II

WHY MILOSEVIC DECIDED TO SETTLE ON JUNE 3

Chapter Four

HE REALIZED THAT HIS HOPED-FOR LEVERAGE ON NATO HAD EVAPORATED

While a number of weeks were to pass before all of Milosevic's assumptions could be fully tested, in the end, none bore out. Indeed, events were to show that Milosevic and his advisers had miscalculated badly. Ethnic cleansing not only did not produce the leverage the Serbs had expected but proved catastrophically counterproductive; NATO's unity and resolve did not erode; and even Russia's diplomatic support for the FRY dissolved at the end.

ETHNIC CLEANSING DID NOT PRODUCE THE LEVERAGE EXPECTED

In all respects, ethnic cleansing failed to produce the results that Serb leaders had hoped would accrue from such operations. Even though it was unable to control territory or protect its civilian support base in Kosovo, the KLA remained a viable organization and a potential military threat in its Albanian sanctuary.[1] Indeed, ethnic cleansing produced a raft of new recruits for the KLA in Albania and opened the pocketbooks of the Albanian diaspora around the world for KLA arms purchases. The KLA's political standing and popularity among the Kosovo Albanians grew as Serb atrocities and despoliation became increasingly widespread.

---

[1]KLA fighters typically took to the hills, sometimes as individuals and sometimes as organized units, when they were confronted by VJ and MUP forces.

Despite the fact that little advance preparation had been made for a massive influx of Kosovo Albanian refugees into Macedonia and Albania, the concerted efforts of the NATO militaries, civilian donor agencies, and nongovernmental organizations (NGOs) managed to contain and eventually alleviate the acute suffering of the refugees.[2] A U.S. airlift to the region, which provided more than one million humanitarian daily rations along with thousands of tents, blankets, and sleeping bags, helped ease the humanitarian crises in Albania and Macedonia during their most acute early days.[3] In the end, neither country was destabilized.

Finally and most significantly, the decision to conduct massive ethnic cleansing and forcefully push hundreds of thousands of refugees into Albania and Macedonia turned out to be a political blunder of enormous magnitude. Instead of strengthening Belgrade's bargaining position, the cleansing seriously weakened it by greatly strengthening NATO's cohesion and resolve. Milosevic's decision to openly drive the Kosovo Albanians out of the country showed his weakness as a strategist—for the cleansing gave the lie to his claim that the FRY was the passive victim of unwarranted NATO aggression.

The revulsion caused by the plight of the refugees streaming out of Kosovo, along with the reports of large-scale executions and hun-

---

[2]According to a U.S. government interagency case study of the humanitarian response to the 1999 refugee crisis,

> U.S. policymakers, intelligence officers, regional experts and humanitarians, along with their counterparts in other NATO member countries, failed to predict until just several days before the bombing campaign that Serb forces would systematically expel Kosovars. Instead, the prevailing worst case scenario was that one million Kosovars would be displaced internally, prohibited from exiting, and remain largely inaccessible, in the context of an ongoing air war and a NATO determination not to launch a ground invasion. The USG was significantly constrained by intelligence deficiencies, especially as regards Milosevic's war strategy and the numbers and calculations of internally displaced Kosovars. This became far worse with the withdrawal of external monitors and relief workers just prior to the onset of the NATO bombing campaign.

See Annex I, "Kosovo Case Study," Interagency Review of U.S. Government Civilian Humanitarian and Transition Programs, U.S. Department of State, January 2000, pp. 1–2, 7–8.

[3]See Major General Larry J. Lust, "Kosovo Campaign Logistics," ECJ4 Log Briefing, Headquarters, United States European Command, July 1999.

dreds of thousands of additional displaced persons within the province, muted the potentially show-stopping concerns of the NATO publics and their political leaders about the legitimacy of the bombing and the civilian human and materiel toll it was extracting. The specter of refugees being moved by trains evoked memories of the Holocaust and strengthened the willingness of wavering coalition partners such as the Greens in Germany to sanction continued attacks. As one Western official put it:

> It is a real question, whether in the absence of ethnic cleansing, NATO would have been able to keep [the bombing] up after a couple of weeks. In a sense [Milosevic's] brutality saved the alliance."[4]

In addition, the creation of massive refugee populations in Albania and Kosovo served to stiffen the terms NATO required for a viable settlement. NATO had no option but to insist on terms that would encourage the refugees to return to Kosovo once the conflict ended. In order to convince the Kosovo Albanian refugees to return home, it was imperative that all Serb military and security forces be made to withdraw from the province.[5] To reassure the refugees, it was also necessary that NATO both command and provide the bulk of the military forces that would implement any agreement. These conditions also made it more likely that the KLA would agree to disarm and demobilize its forces.

Finally, by expelling the Kosovo Albanians from Kosovo, the Serbs made it possible for NATO governments and NGOs to provide humanitarian support to most of the victims of the ethnic cleansing. Had the Serbs confined their operations to creating only IDPs, NATO might have been pressured to soften its terms for a settlement in order to ward off a humanitarian disaster it otherwise could not help alleviate.[6] In any event, confining the refugees to Kosovo would have

---

[4]Cohen, July 2, 1999, pp. A1 and A8.

[5]See "Clinton's Remarks in Defense of Military Intervention in Balkans," *New York Times*, May 14, 1999, p. A12.

[6]At one point, NATO planners considered employing 24 daily sorties of C-130s to drop 90,000 humanitarian daily rations per day to IDPs within Kosovo using the Tri-wall Aerial Delivery System (TRIADS) from various altitudes. NATO leaders ruled out this air drop option apparently on the grounds that it would prove too risky given Serb air defense capabilities. The air drop plan is described in Lust, July 1999.

greatly reduced the media's ability to convincingly portray and document what was going on inside Kosovo. This would have made it more difficult for the NATO governments to justify continued air attacks both to their citizens and to the international community at large.

NATO REMAINED UNITED AND RESOLUTE

Milosevic's hopes that the international public would "rebel" against continued bombing and that NATO's unity would be sundered once NATO air strikes began to take a toll of civilian casualties went unrealized. The Serbian leader clearly failed to anticipate how the Western European public's abhorrence of ethnic cleansing might trump its concerns about civilian victims of the bombing.

A May 28, 1999, article by the Yugoslav Army Supreme Command Headquarters Information Service shows how thoroughly the Serbs had become disabused of any hope that international public opinion would come to their aid:

> The repeated warnings that the attacks on the electric power and water supply systems are violating the basic norms of the international law and humane principles, and that they are depriving the civilian population of all the elementary living conditions, are leaving the international public totally indifferent. They are obviously set by the media to emotionally react only to the suffering of Albanian refugees. The torment of 10,000,000 Yugoslav citizens does not concern them very much. This is why the dark forces of NATO are allowed to pursue the daily destruction of a sovereign state, without the declaration of war and without the approval of the UN Security Council.[7]

The comparatively passive reaction that greeted the massive ethnic cleansing of Serbs by Croat forces in 1995 may have misled Milosevic about the likely international response to ethnic cleansing. Milosevic, in an April 1999 interview, commented on the fact that the

---

[7]See Yugoslav Army Supreme Command Headquarters—Information Service, "Forces of Dark," Press Center, May 28, 1999.

expulsion of 500,000 Serbs from Croatia had been "ignored by the world media."[8]

After the war, senior Yugoslav officials privately confirmed that they had badly misjudged NATO's resolve and that the decision to defy NATO had been based on a "terrible miscalculation." One high-ranking Serb official summarized this misjudgment as follows:

> We never thought NATO would stay united through 10 weeks of bombing and the killing of innocent civilians. We convinced ourselves it would have split open weeks ago."[9]

Another senior official said that the Serbs had expected France to break ranks with the United States when civilian casualties began to mount. The official added, however, that "we got it all wrong."[10]

Belgrade's efforts to split the Alliance were undermined by the measure adopted by NATO to limit allied casualties and minimize civilian casualties and collateral damage. Prior to clearing a potential fixed target for attack, allied authorities attempted to ascertain the likely civilian casualties that might result from the strike. Targets estimated to generate high civilian casualties were withheld from attack. NATO airmen attempted to design optimum strike modes that would limit possible collateral damage from the strikes on the targets that were cleared for attack. When particular target sets or modes of attack produced unanticipated civilian casualties, NATO commanders tightened their rules of engagement (ROE) so as to reduce the chances that similar unwanted casualties would occur in the future.

Milosevic's hopes of imposing costs on NATO by downing large numbers of NATO aircraft and gaining bargaining leverage by capturing pilots were also unrealized. The some 845 surface-to-air missiles (SAMs) that FRY forces fired at NATO aircraft during the course of the campaign brought down only two manned aircraft, and these without the loss of pilots.[11] An expert combat search-and-

---

[8]See de Borchgrave, May 1, 1999, p. 8.

[9]See de Borchgrave, June 11, 1999, p. 1.

[10]Ibid.

[11]In addition to the F-117 and F-16 that were downed by enemy missiles, the NATO allies also lost some 25 unmanned aerial vehicles (UAVs) during the air campaign. See

rescue (CSAR) operation prevented the capture of a downed F-117 pilot in Serbia. The NATO commanders were able to minimize their losses of manned aircraft mainly by flying at altitudes beyond antiaircraft artillery (AAA) and shoulder-fired missile range, using stealth aircraft and standoff missiles to attack targets in high-risk defense areas, and employing extensive suppression of enemy air defense (SEAD) operations during air attacks.[12]

The conviction of many of the allies that the very future of NATO was at stake in the outcome of the conflict also served to solidify the NATO governments' resolve to persevere until their terms were met. Milosevic's attempts to secure a bombing halt prior to an agreement failed, as did his attempts to entice NATO governments into accepting one or more of his peace ploys.[13] The troop withdrawal and peace enforcement terms offered by Belgrade always fell far short of what NATO required to ensure the return of the refugees and the disarmament of the KLA.

RUSSIA'S SUPPORT FOR THE FRY DISSOLVED

Milosevic and his colleagues were also disabused of the hope that Russia could be drawn more deeply into the conflict and would be willing and able to exert sufficient pressure on NATO to cause the Alliance to halt the bombing or significantly soften its terms for war termination.

Any expectations the Serbs may have harbored about any direct Russian military support were soon confounded by Yeltsin's repeated public and private pledges to eschew Russian military involvement. Yeltsin undoubtedly recognized that any direct military intervention or arms resupply on behalf of the Serbs would be both difficult and dangerous. Russia's power projection capabilities were extremely limited, and the land and air routes to Serbia were con-

---

William M. Arkin, "Top Air Force Leaders to Get Briefed on Serbia Air War Report," *Defense Daily*, June 13, 2000, p. 1.

[12]Even though the Serbs used their radars sparingly, some 743 high-speed antiradiation missiles (HARMs) were launched against FRY radars by U.S. and allied aircraft. See Arkin, June 13, 2000, p. 1.

[13]At different points in the air campaign, Greece and Italy unsuccessfully urged NATO to observe a brief bombing pause to test Belgrade's willingness to negotiate.

trolled by countries that supported the NATO effort. Moscow's only direct access to the FRY was limited to sea supply through Montenegro's Adriatic ports, which were vulnerable to blockade and interdiction. American officials had warned Russian leaders early on in the conflict that "any effort by them to intervene in a militarily significant way could have very serious consequences."[14] Yeltsin was determined not to be dragged into a war with NATO over Kosovo.

While some Moscow foreign policy and military officials may have considered Milosevic to be Russia's "main partner in the Balkans," Yeltsin was unwilling to risk a military confrontation with NATO to ensure Milosevic's continued tenure as leader of the FRY or to ensure Serb control of Kosovo. Milosevic had hardly endeared himself to Yeltsin by supporting the 1991 coup by communist hard-liners in Moscow. More significantly, Milosevic's practice of generating one conflict after another in the former Yugoslavia had worked against Moscow's interests, as it had drawn NATO forces successively deeper into the Balkans.[15] Oleg Levitin, a former Russian foreign ministry official involved in Moscow's Balkan policies in 1990–1999, writes that "the clearest illustration of Milosevic's low ratings in Moscow was the fact that Yeltsin never paid his promised visit to Yugoslavia, and never accepted Milosevic on a state visit to Russia."[16] As a member of the Contact Group, Russia had helped negotiate the Rambouillet accord and probably would have been content to have seen Serbia sign the agreement.[17]

From Yeltsin's standpoint, the confrontation with NATO over Kosovo was counterproductive to Moscow's primary diplomatic and eco-

---

[14]Michael R. Gordon, "U.S. Warns Russia: Don't Provide Help to Serbian Military," *New York Times*, April 10, 1999, pp. A1 and A8.

[15]In his memoirs, Yeltsin described Milosevic as "one of the most cynical politicians I have ever dealt with." Yeltsin, 2000, p. 265.

[16]According to Levitin, prior to the NATO air campaign, Moscow feared that Milosevic might either "abuse his relationship with Russia to cause further friction between Moscow and the West" or, alternatively, "strike a deal behind Russia's back" that would undermine Moscow's prestige both at home and abroad. Levitin attributes Moscow's continued willingness to consider Milosevic its "main partner in the Balkans" to the "anti-Western feelings, spheres-of-influences aspirations, and, above all, inertia" of senior Russian foreign ministry officials. See Levitin, Spring 2000, pp. 133–135.

[17]Op. cit., pp. 136–137.

nomic interests.[18] Yeltsin needed good relations with the West if he was to secure the money, technology, and expertise needed for the rebuilding of Russia.[19] Among other near-term needs, Moscow required additional International Monetary Fund (IMF) money to avoid default on its IMF loans and wanted private Western lenders to reschedule some $31 billion in bad debt.[20] Achieving closure on these issues would have proved difficult, if not impossible, while the fighting continued.

However, Yeltsin was under pressure to do something in response to the bombing.[21] To deflect domestic pressures for a Russian military involvement, Yeltsin reverted to tough Cold War–style oratory to condemn the bombing and ordered a series of punitive diplomatic steps that temporarily severed Russia's formal relations with NATO.[22] Yet Moscow's only military move was to deploy an intelligence collection vessel to an area just south of the Adriatic to monitor NATO operations.[23]

To speed a negotiated end to the war, Yeltsin dispatched Chernomyrdin to broker an agreement. During his shuttle diplomacy, Chernomyrdin attempted both to soften NATO's terms and to wring concessions from Milosevic.[24] Progress on the core issues that

---

[18]After the conflict, Yeltsin declared that Russia's number one strategic interest was to restore relations with the West.

[19]See Roland Dannreuther, "Escaping the Enlargement Trap in NATO-Russian Relations," *Survival*, Winter 1999, p. 148.

[20]See Michael Wines, "Russia and NATO, Split over Kosovo, Agree to Renew Relations," *New York Times*, February 17, 2000, p. A11.

[21]Among other things, Yeltsin's communist opponents, "emboldened by the anti-Western mood" in Russia, had been pressing for an impeachment vote in the Duma against the president. Bohlen, April 10, 1999, p. A8.

[22]Moscow withdrew its mission from Brussels, suspended its participation in the Partnership for Peace and the Founding Act, terminated discussions on the establishment of a NATO military mission in Moscow, and ordered the NATO information officer in Moscow to leave the country. See Oksana Antonenko, "Russia, NATO and European Security After Kosovo," *Survival*, Winter 1999, p. 131.

[23]Gordon, April 10, 1999, pp. A1 and A8.

[24]Strobe Talbott described Chernomyrdin's role as that of a "hammer" that "would pound away on Milosevic." Chernomyrdin, on the other hand, saw his diplomacy as advancing Russia's interest in settling the war by extracting compromises from both sides. He told Talbott, "If you want to persuade Milosevic you have to convince me first." Talbott confirms that the Russians required considerable persuading. See In-

were in dispute was glacial during the early weeks of the negotiations as Milosevic resisted agreeing to major concessions and Chernomyrdin, acting under Yeltsin's instructions, remained unwilling to accede to NATO's key bottom-line demands that all Serb forces be withdrawn from the province and that a NATO-led military presence in Kosovo with "substantial" NATO participation be introduced to keep the peace.[25] This negotiating impasse suddenly dissolved in the first days of June, when Moscow broke ranks with Belgrade and agreed to endorse NATO's terms for war termination.[26]

A key reason for this shift in Moscow's position seems to have been the Russian belief that a NATO invasion of the FRY was in the offing.[27] Early on in the conflict, Yeltsin had manifested a particular

---

terview with former Deputy Secretary of State Strobe Talbott and Interview with Viktor Chernomyrdin for PBS *Frontline*, "War in Europe," February 22, 2000, and Stabile, June 10, 1999.

[25]Commenting on Yeltsin's control of the negotiations, Chernomyrdin stated, "I performed my tasks under President Yeltsin's directives and in full coordination with Foreign Minister Ivanov. Every sentence, every reply, every comma was agreed on." See Stabile, June 10, 1999. See also William Drozdiak, "The Kosovo Peace Deal: How It Happened," *Washington Post*, June 6, 1999, p. A1.

[26]Talbott reports that the Russians conceded on the pivotal NATO demand that "all" Serb forces be withdrawn from Kosovo only on the morning of June 2, shortly before Chernomyrdin and Ahtisaari were scheduled to fly to Belgrade. See Interview with Strobe Talbott, February 22, 2000.

[27]A question naturally arises as to whether Russian officials actually believed that a NATO invasion was in the offing or were simply using this threat to pressure Milosevic into making concessions. Yeltsin writes that "Chernomyrdin's main purpose was to try to press Milosevic to conduct peace talks with the West," a task he "pushed hard, letting Milosevic know that he could expect no military support and that his political support was already exhausted" (Yeltsin, 2000, p. 264). At the time the Kosovo conflict ended, NATO clearly still lacked both the political consensus and the force posture in the theater needed for an invasion. At the earliest, a NATO ground assault was still two to three months away. However, Yeltsin reveals in his memoirs that as early as April 22, Moscow officials had become "alarmed" by the reports that NATO planned to conduct a ground operation in Kosovo, a course of action that they believed would be "the path to the abyss" (Yeltsin, 2000, p. 261). There seems to have been an attempt on the part of U.S. and UK officials to hype the threat of an invasion. As noted below, Secretary Talbott did not discourage the belief that a ground attack was being prepared. Indeed, there may have been an attempt to encourage a perception among the Russians and the Serbs that planning was further along the road than it was (Ben Barber, "Milosevic May Have Been Spooked into Leaving Kosovo," *Washington Times*, July 20, 1999, p. A15). Poor intelligence analysis may also have facilitated Moscow's misreading of NATO's plans and capabilities. During periods of the Cold War, shoddy and distorted Soviet intelligence analyses grossly misinformed the Moscow leadership about U.S. military intentions, claiming, for example, that the United States was

concern about NATO's possible use of ground forces and had specifically warned the allies not to invade the FRY.[28] A ground attack would have put Yeltsin under great domestic pressure to do something to actively assist the Serbs militarily. At a minimum, a ground invasion would have forced a deeper and more lasting rupture with the West, endangering Western credits, investment, and cooperation for some time to come.

By late May, senior Russian officials apparently had become convinced that a NATO ground invasion was looming. Russian Foreign Minister Igor Ivanov stated in an interview with *Newsweek* that Moscow "had reliable information that preparation for a ground operation was in full swing."[29] Chernomyrdin, perhaps as a consequence of his conversations with Secretary Talbott, also seems to have believed that an invasion was in the offing.[30] In defending his role as peacemaker, he implied that such a land campaign could have provoked a Russian confrontation with NATO that would have brought the world to "the brink of a total conflagration."[31]

The perceived threat of a ground attack persuaded Yeltsin, for his own ends, to seek a quick end to the conflict. As a former Russian foreign ministry official put it:

---

preparing to launch a first strike against the USSR. See Christopher Andrew, "The Mitrokhin Archive," *RUSI Journal*, February 2000, pp. 55–56.

[28]On April 9, in a television appearance, Yeltsin unmistakably warned NATO not to push Russia into war: "I told NATO, the Americans, the Germans, don't push us toward military action, otherwise there will be a European war for sure, and possibly a world war. We are against this." Later in the day, Yeltsin set down a more explicit marker concerning future NATO actions in the Balkans: "They [NATO] want to use ground troops, take over Yugoslavia, make it their protectorate. We cannot allow this. Russia and the access to the Mediterranean Sea are nearby, so we can by no means give Yugoslavia away." See Bohlen, April 10, 1999, p. A8.

[29]See "NATO's Game of Chicken," *Newsweek*, July 26, 1999, p. 60.

[30]Talbott reveals that he made a concerted effort to convey to Chernomyrdin— "because the Russians were talking to the Yugoslav leadership the whole time"—that the ground invasion option had not been taken off the table. "We wanted to make sure that the issue of ground troops was primarily going to translate into pressure on Milosevic to say Uncle." See Interview with Strobe Talbott, February 22, 2000.

[31]See Stabile, June 10, 1999.

Only the assumption that a NATO ground operation was imminent convinced Moscow to play a constructive role in June 1999, negotiating an international NATO-led military presence in Kosovo.[32]

Russia's endorsement of NATO's terms constituted a severe blow to the Serbs, who now saw themselves as isolated and vulnerable to greatly intensified NATO bombing. Senior Serb officials, along with a number of Russian military leaders, openly characterized the Russian action as a "sell-out."[33] One senior Serb official confessed that the Belgrade leaders had badly miscalculated when they assumed Russia would sustain its diplomatic support for the FRY, saying, "We should have realized Russia would betray us."[34]

---

[32]Levitin, Spring 2000, p. 138.

[33]General Leonid Ivashov, who accompanied Chernomyrdin and represented Russia's Ministry of Defense at the peace talks, openly assailed the June 3 agreement as a "sell-out to the West." See Vladimir Isachenkov, "Russian General Openly Questions NATO Deal on Kosovo," *Washington Times*, June 10, 1999, p. A14.

[34]See de Borchgrave, June 11, 1999.

Chapter Five

BOMBING PRODUCED A POPULAR CLIMATE
CONDUCIVE TO CONCESSIONS

As noted earlier, Milosevic's initial decision to reject NATO's ultimatum regarding Kosovo stemmed from the belief that a posture of defiance would enhance his political standing among the Serbs and best ensure his continued hold on power. Serb public opinion in mid-March of 1999 was strongly "hawkish" on Kosovo, and Milosevic clearly believed it too risky to make major concessions without it appearing that he had been compelled to do so or without a significant erosion of the then-prevailing public and elite sentiment to defend the province "at any cost."[1] According to Chernomyrdin, "Milosevic in particular" was concerned about the public's perception of any settlement: he wanted to appear to be a "winner" and "justify [himself] before his own nation."[2]

One of the most important effects of the NATO bombing campaign was to produce a political climate within Serbia that was conducive to major concessions on Kosovo. By the end of the campaign, the Serbian citizens and political leaders who had initially opposed giving in to NATO's demands had increasingly come to the view that Milosevic must do whatever was necessary to get the bombing stopped.

---

[1] See "Opinion Poll," March 18, 1999.

[2] Interview with Viktor Chernomyrdin, PBS *Frontline*, "War in Europe," February 22, 2000.

THE INITIAL PUBLIC REACTION TO THE BOMBING WAS SURPRISE AND ANGRY DEFIANCE

Despite the threats of NATO military action that followed the collapse of the negotiations over Kosovo, it seems that major elements of the Serbian public did not expect bombing. In the *Nin* opinion poll, conducted 11 days before the start of hostilities, almost 80 percent of the respondents indicated that they did not believe there would be bombing.[3] And when asked who would win in the event Serbia did clash with NATO, more respondents (46 percent) thought Serbia would prevail than thought NATO would win (28 percent).[4]

Serbian public support for Milosevic and his refusal to accede to NATO's ultimatum over Kosovo seemed to be strengthened, if anything, by the first weeks of attack. The initial popular reaction in Serbia to the NATO cruise missile strikes and bombing was angry defiance. Public fear and anxiety about the bombing clearly seemed to be outweighed by a growing outrage over the attacks, which triggered a surge of Serbian nationalist sentiment across the country:[5]

> Faced with a foreign assault, the people rallied around Milosevic and mocked Western claims that NATO had no quarrel with the Serbian people but only with their leaders. Milosevic calculated—correctly as it turned out, at least in the short run—that the spectacle of a leader uncompromisingly rejecting a foreign ultimatum fitted the nation's psyche, much as Lazar had refused to accommodate the Turks in 1389. There arose a wave of patriotic euphoria which projected Milosevic as the leader of a united people embarked on a holy cause. The nation's top military commander, speaking in the language of the myth, told his troops to "prepare for martyrdom."[6]

---

[3]In *Nin's* telephone poll of 200 randomly selected Serbian citizens, 78.5 percent of the respondents said they did not expect bombing and 76 percent said they believed the problems of Kosovo could be resolved through political negotiations. See "Opinion Poll," March 18, 1999.

[4]Some 14 percent of the respondents said there would be no winning side, while 11.5 percent said they did not know. See "Opinion Poll," March 18, 1999.

[5]Guy Dinmore, "Daily Life in Belgrade Teeters Under Strikes," *Washington Post*, April 5, 1999, p. A1.

[6]Doder and Branson, 1999, pp. 8–9.

The eruption of patriotic sentiment was manifest in the daily "rock and bomb" concerts that began to be held throughout Serbia. By the first week of April, as many as 100,000 people, young and old alike, were gathering in Belgrade's Republic Square to sing, dance to rock music, wave anti-NATO placards, and listen to poetry readings that aimed to showcase the Serb's cultural superiority. Similar daily anti-NATO concerts were held in other major cities throughout the country, where protesters carrying posters of Milosevic, chanted, "Slobo! Slobo!"[7]

Popular defiance toward the NATO attacks was also symbolized by the black-and-white bull's-eye targets that "multiplied like a virus" throughout the country during the first weeks of the bombing. Designed to mock NATO's claims that it had "no quarrel with the Serbian people, only with their leaders," the sign could be seen everywhere adorning billboards, bridges, newspaper front pages, and the lapels of government officials and television anchors.[8] Serbia's government-controlled media sought to maximize the public's patriotic outrage over the bombing while at the same time attempting to "minimize the public's fear that any harm would befall them personally."[9]

A rally-around-the-flag effect was also manifest among Milosevic's political opponents as criticism of the FRY president became muted. Most opposition politicians had fully supported Serbian rejection of the Rambouillet accords and were in no position to criticize the consequences of that action.[10] The opposition leaders, whose political identity was closely tied to the West and who had led the country-wide demonstrations against Milosevic in 1997, saw their positions gravely weakened and Milosevic's strengthened by the bombing. As

---

[7]See Guy Dinmore, "NATO Destroys Major Bridge," *Washington Post*, April 4, 1999, p. A12; Dinmore, April 5, 1999, p. A11; and Aleksander Ciric, "Comment: It's a Serbian Thing," *Institute for War and Peace Reporting*, April 15, 1999, http://iwpr.vs4. cerbernet.co.uk/index.pl?archive/bcr/bcr_19990415_1_eng.txt.

[8]Michael Dobbs, "Serbs' Bull's-Eyes Defy, Mock NATO," *Washington Post*, April 9, 1999, p. A1, and Ciric, April 15, 1999.

[9]Ciric, April 15, 1999.

[10]See Sonya Biserko, "Comment: The Belgrade Stranglehold," *Institute for War and Peace Reporting*, February 11, 2000, http://iwpr.vs4.cerbernet.co.uk/index.pl?archive/bcr/bcr_20000211_3_eng.txt.

Zoran Djindjic, the leader of the opposition Democratic Party, put it: "The biggest loser in this war is my Party. . . . Our entire political identity is closely tied to Europe and America. For most people here, Europe has become identical with NATO, which is identical with bombs."[11] Capitulation to NATO's demands in this initial climate of patriotic fervor would have cost Milosevic this newly found political support and possibly his rule.

AFTER A MONTH OF BOMBING, PUBLIC ATTITUDES BEGAN TO CHANGE

As the bombing continued, however, the mood in the country began to change. By early May, people were reportedly focusing increasingly on issues of daily survival and began to realize "that they were in for a long and difficult period and that things were likely to get worse."[12]

By the third week in May, there were increasing manifestations that Serbians had become deeply weary of the war. The change in sentiment was palpable. The audiences at the daily rock concerts in downtown Belgrade had dwindled from 100,000 to a few dozen—and the only reason the concerts were still held was that officials had promised they would continue until the bombing stopped. The once heavily promoted nighttime rallies on Belgrade's bridges that had been sponsored by the political party of Mirjana Markovic, the wife of President Milosevic, no longer took place at all.[13]

Interviews showed that while many of Belgrade's citizens still believed in the rightness of their cause and were proud of "their brave if inevitably futile defense against all the might of NATO," they were nevertheless anxious for the war to come to an end. As one reporter

---

[11]Michael Dobbs, "NATO Bombing Campaign Wounds Milosevic's Political Enemies," *Washington Post*, April 13, 1999, p. A19.

[12]The change in mood was clearly manifest in Novi Sad, a Serbian city of 300,000 that had suffered disruptions of electric power, water supply, and telephone service. Local journalists in Novi Sad, however, reportedly did not see people as yet "moving to press the Government to yield to NATO's conditions." See Carlotta Gall, "No Water, Power, Phone: A Serbian City's Trials," *New York Times*, May 4, 1999, p. A12.

[13]Steven Erlanger, "Belgrade's People Still Defiant, but Deeply Weary," *New York Times*, May 24, 1999, p. A1.

described prevailing attitudes, the population anticipated a political settlement that would bring foreign troops into Kosovo and expressed frustration that "it was taking so long to write down the obvious." They expressed the fear that people were "dying for the reputation of politicians on both sides" and that NATO would "somehow double the stakes" as it continued to "bomb hospitals, bridges, and power stations."[14]

By early June, people seemed "exhausted and demoralized by the NATO air strikes." The energy that had galvanized Serbs into an outpouring of popular rage and defiance at the NATO bombing during the early weeks of the war had dissipated into a struggle for personal survival.[15]

These changes in popular attitudes were conditioned by three effects of the bombing: (1) the immediate physical hardships it caused individual Serbian citizens, (2) the fears it generated among the public about their own safety and the safety of their loved ones, and (3) the anxieties it engendered among the public about the vicissitudes they were likely to face in the future. These concerns intensified as the bombing became prolonged and increasingly embraced a larger array of infrastructure targets, such as bridges, refineries, and electric power grids.

Bombing Caused Physical Hardships for the Public

Five weeks into the air campaign, many Serbs were reporting some form of personal hardship as a result of the bombing. A wartime public opinion poll, conducted at the beginning of May by Belgrade's Institute for Policy Studies, disclosed that some 71 percent of the Serbian citizens questioned reported suffering privations caused by shortages of certain goods. Some 42 percent of citizens 18 or older said they had been forced "to leave their homes to move to a safer location." No fewer than 96 percent of the respondents reported suf-

---

[14]Ibid. See also George Jahn, "Desperation Takes Over Belgrade," Associated Press, May 1, 1999.

[15]Michael Dobbs, "Despairing Serbs Struggle for Survival," *Washington Post*, reprinted in *Manchester Guardian Weekly*, June 27, 1999, p. 15.

fering from "psychological problems caused by worry for their future and the future of their families."[16]

Attacks on Serbia's electric generating system caused particularly severe hardships, as the resulting power shutdowns often denied the public both electricity and running water. While contending that the strikes on infrastructure targets had legitimate military-related purposes, NATO officials also acknowledged that the attacks were aimed in part at damaging the quality of life so that suffering citizens would start questioning the intransigence of their political leadership.[17] Lieutenant General Short, the NATO air component commander, hoped that the distress of the Yugoslav public would undermine support for the authorities in Belgrade.[18]

Beyond these direct privations, however, the NATO bombing also caused other side effects that were "numerous, varied, and multiplying by the day."[19] Household staples—such as oil, sugar, washing soap, and diapers—became more expensive and harder to obtain. The lines for cigarettes, which had doubled in price, wound farther and farther back from the few street kiosks that still had supplies. Travel between towns, for those who could afford it, became increasingly difficult. Some trips that had once taken one or two hours now took nine or ten.[20] To save money, the government closed schools and cut its monthly payments to pensioners by half.[21] Hundreds of

---

[16]Since the poll's methodology, the size and makeup of its sample, and its margin of error are unknown to the author, the percentages cited above must be viewed with caution. The poll's results were reported in "Harsh Reality Under the Bombs," *Institute for War and Peace Reporting,* June 3, 1999, http://iwpr.vs4.cerbernet.co.uk/index.pl?archive/bcr/bcr_19990603_3_eng.txt. The author of the article was described as "an independent journalist from Belgrade whose identity has been concealed."

[17]See Philip Bennett and Steve Coll, "NATO Warplanes Jolt Yugoslav Power Grid," *Washington Post,* May 25, 1999, pp. A1 and A11.

[18]See Michael R. Gordon, "Allied Air Chief Stresses Hitting Belgrade Sites," *New York Times,* May 13, 1999, pp. A1 and A11.

[19]See Philippa Fletcher, "NATO Air Strikes Lead to Tough Times for Serbs," *Washington Times,* May 12, 1999, p. A12.

[20]Some 72 percent of the respondents in the Institute for Policy Studies poll reported being directly inconvenienced by the destruction of bridges and roads.

[21]See Fletcher, May 12, 1999; Jean Baptiste Naudet, "'We're All Going Crazy Here, We're on Pills,'" *Le Monde,* May 25, 1999, reprinted in *Manchester Guardian Weekly,* June 6, 1999, p. 13; and an anonymous senior columnist in Belgrade, "National Unity:

thousands of Serbs were without jobs after NATO aircraft struck many of the country's industrial plants.[22] The Institute for Policy Studies poll revealed that more than half of those who had formerly been counted among the "officially" employed in Serbia either had lost their jobs or were no longer working because of the war.[23]

Bombing Caused Stress and Concerns About Personal and Family Safety

The NATO air operations over Serbia and Kosovo also eventually engendered severe anxiety among the Serbian citizenry about their own safety and the safety of loved ones, including the troops deployed in Kosovo. Even though the NATO allies went to extraordinary lengths to minimize civilian casualties and made a major effort in their public statements and psychological operation (PSYOP) broadcasts and leaflet drops to reassure Serbians that the bombing was not directed at the civilian population, many Serbs apparently believed the opposite. They became convinced that NATO's bombing errors were not errors at all but were part of a psychological warfare campaign to "demoralize the people." As one reporter described it:

> NATO missiles have largely been so precise that many Serbs no longer believe that NATO ever bombs in error, even if the damage is to the Chinese Embassy or a hospital.[24]

The perception of deliberate attacks on civilian targets was reinforced by the constant attention devoted on the regime-controlled television to instances of collateral damage:

> The only TV pictures are of NATO's horrific "blunders"—broken bodies and shattered buses, trains and hospitals—which are repeated endlessly until they become meaningless. Then another

---

Utter Exhaustion," *Institute for War and Peace Reporting,* May 21, 1999, http://iwpr.vs4.cerbernet.co.uk/index.pl?archive/bcr/bcr_19990521_2_eng.txt.

[22]Dobbs, June 27, 1999, p. 15.

[23]"Harsh Reality Under the Bombs," June 3, 1999.

[24]Erlanger, May 24, 1999, pp. A1, A14.

blunder comes along that gives this macabre propaganda a new lease of life.[25]

The threat of constant air raids—magnified by numerous false alarms from an inadequate air raid warning system—took its toll on the Serbian population. Because Serbia is a small country with many potential target areas located in close proximity, the FRY personnel operating the air raid warning net had difficulty differentiating where incoming NATO aircraft intended to strike. In Belgrade, which was only infrequently hit by NATO air strikes, air raid sirens sounded every day. According to the official statistics of the City Alert Centre, Belgrade's citizens experienced no fewer than 146 air raid warnings during the 78-day bombing campaign. Air raid alerts lasted for a total of 774 hours, which meant that citizens taking cover during all warnings would have spent an average of 9 hours and 55 minutes a day in shelters.[26] There were only three nights when air raid warnings did not sound.

The citizens of Novi Sad also experienced numerous air raid warnings. One journalist, writing in early May, described the situation as follows:

> At the beginning of the bombing campaign, air raid sirens wailed every day at nightfall. But there are no longer any rules. Sometimes the siren wails in the middle of the day, sometimes in the middle of the night. Not all citizens react in the same way. Some go down into the shelters, some sit at home, and some in cafes. . . . But all citizens of Novi Sad frequently ask the same two questions: Why is the bombing of their city happening? And how long will it last?[27]

Many Serbians experienced months of sleep deprivation—remaining awake at night during the bombings and sleeping by day. In Belgrade, the perception that NATO was attacking civilian targets

---

[25]Naudet, May 25, 1999.

[26]The longest air raid alert lasted 23 hours and 15 minutes on March 31–April 1. The shortest alert lasted only 19 minutes on April 16. See Yugoslav Army Supreme Command Headquarters—Information Service, "774 Hours of Air Raids in Belgrade," Press Center, June 17, 1999.

[27]See Milena Putnik, "Broken Bridges, Disrupted Lives," *Institute for War and Peace Reporting*, May 4, 1999, http://iwpr.vs4.cerbernet.co.uk/index.pl?archive/bcr/bcr_19990504_1_eng.txt.

caused many people "to spend every night in air raid shelters."[28] Instances of suicide and mental depression increased, and many citizens of Belgrade suffered from an exaggerated "startle response," whereby any loud noises made them jump or flinch.[29]

The stress of the bombing was compounded by the invisibility of the attacker. As one Serbian Red Cross psychologist described it: "This is a special kind of war. You never see the enemy, so you feel helpless." Psychologist Jelena Vlajkovic reported that the Red Cross received up to 30 calls a day from Belgraders who felt they were on the verge of mental breakdown as a result of the bombing. Other residents showed the physical effects of stress: insomnia, shortness of breath, stomach cramps. The propensity of Serbs to engage in gallows humor about the bombing at one moment and breakdown in tears at another was, according to Vlajkovic, a manifestation of their need to both distance themselves from the war and let off pressure.[30]

Stress from the bombing was also prevalent in other areas of the country. A French reporter recounted being confronted during his travels outside Belgrade by a Serbian journalist who exclaimed:

> "Don't you realize we're all going crazy here? Everyone is on pills. . .
> He took out a box of tranquilizers that he kept in his pocket. "It's the result of the bombing," he added.[31]

CONCERNS ABOUT CASUALTIES PROVOKED ANTIWAR DEMONSTRATIONS IN MILOSEVIC'S "HEARTLAND"

While the personnel losses in the Yugoslav Army caused by the bombing or ground engagements with the KLA were probably modest, popular concerns about actual and potential future casualties among the troops deployed in Kosovo prompted antiwar protests.

---

[28]See "National Unity: Utter Exhaustion," May 21, 1999.

[29]William Booth, "Bombs Broke Hearts and Minds: In Yugoslavia, Lasting Damage Will Be Psychological," *Washington Post*, July 17, 1999, p. A13.

[30]See Marcus Gee, "Jokes, Tears Help Serbs Cope with Raids," *Washington Times*, June 2, 1999, p. A8.

[31]Naudet, May 25, 1999.

The feelings of fear and frustration felt by many Serbs during the conflict were intensified by the prolonged absence of men—particularly in the south of Serbia, where many of the draftees and reservists whom the government had mobilized and sent to Kosovo lived.[32] The prolonged absences, along with the concerns family members harbored about the safety of the troops in Kosovo, eventually spawned antiwar demonstrations in a number of south-central Serbian towns.

The deaths of ten local reservists who had been serving in Kosovo and the lack of information about when their sons would be demobilized led hundreds of soldiers' mothers in the Serbian towns of Krusevac, Aleksandrovac, and Trstenik to stage demonstrations demanding that their sons be returned home from their army service in Kosovo. The demonstrations were sparked in part by Milosevic's announcement that troops were being withdrawn from Kosovo now that the "terrorists" had been successfully suppressed, and the families were angry that their sons had still not come home.[33] The theme of the protests, which apparently arose spontaneously, was summarized in the slogan "We want sons, not coffins." Demonstrators reportedly also chanted "Give us our children back" and "We want peace!"[34]

As one Belgrade journalist described the situation, the protesters

> . . . do not wish to see Serbia surrender Kosovo, nor do they wish to topple Milosevic. They just want Belgrade to seek a political solution and agree to a settlement as soon as possible, no matter how humiliating the terms.[35]

---

[32]See "Two Months of Air Campaign Against Yugoslavia," BETA, May 27, 1999, *FBIS* translated text, FTS19990527001145.

[33]Carlotta Gall, "Women Protest Draftees' Kosovo Duty," *New York Times*, May 20, 1999, p. A15, and "Protests Are Resumed by Families of Yugoslav Reservists Ordered Back to Duty in Kosovo," *New York Times*, May 25, 1999, p. A17.

[34]See Steven Erlanger, "Yugoslav Politicians Carefully Maneuver for Day Milosevic Is Gone," *New York Times*, May 21, 1999, p. A1, and Gall, May 20, 1999.

[35]See "The Dead Don't Care About Kosovo," *Institute for War and Peace Reporting*, June 3, 1999, http://iwpr.vs4.cerbernet.co.uk/index.pl?archive/bcr/bcr_19990603_4_eng.txt.

The protests in Krusevac took on added import when more than 500 reservists from the Seventh Infantry Brigade that was stationed in Istok, Kosovo, reportedly deserted their positions and fought through a military checkpoint to return to their homes in Krusevac. The troops had apparently heard from Western radio broadcasts that the Serb police were using force to suppress the demonstrators in Krusevac and thus deserted to rescue their families. Belgrade had to send the Third Army Commander, Lieutenant General Pavkovic, to Krusevac to talk to the soldiers and their parents to quiet the situation.[36]

These deserters, along with hundreds of other reservists from the Krusevac area, who were apparently granted a few days' home leave to ease tensions in the town, subsequently refused to return to their units in Kosovo, claiming that the Krusevac region had already provided a disproportionate share of the troops for Kosovo. Many of the reservists also accused the local authorities, particularly officials of the governing Socialist Party, of "showing favoritism and allowing young men with connections to avoid being ordered into active service."[37] On May 23, a crowd of reservists and their families, variously estimated to number between 1000 and 3000 persons, demonstrated in Krusevac against the troops being ordered back to Kosovo. Another crowd of demonstrators, including a number of reservists in uniform, assembled in the nearby town of Aleksandrovac and tried to join the protest in Krusevac but were turned back by the authorities.

According to the account of one Aleksandrovac resident, the reservists from Aleksandrovac feared returning to Kosovo because of the bombing. The resident reported that the soldiers were all "telling one story":

> "Their lives are in danger down there. Planes are flying very low—they don't hit them much: they are targeting mostly armor and military objects—but the men do not see the purpose of being there. They feel like live targets, they feel that NATO can just cover them with bombs any time it wants and they might die for nothing." The

---

[36]See Gall, May 20, 1999; Eric Schmitt, "Hundreds of Yugoslav Troops Said to Desert," *New York Times*, May 20, 1999, p. A15; and *V.I.P Daily News Report 1510*, May 20, 1999, p. 3 and *1512*, May 24, 1999, p. 3.

[37]See Gall, May 25, 1999, and *V.I.P. Daily News Report 1512*, May 24, 1999, pp. 3–4.

resident said that the troops who returned had said they no longer felt as safe in Kosovo as they did earlier. "This is not a political protest," he said. "It is simply people who are trying to save their necks."[38]

Serb authorities subsequently banned all further demonstrations in the area and detained some reservists for failing to report to their war units.[39]

Similar antiwar protests were reported in the towns of Brus, Raska, and Paljevic. Villagers in Raska and Paljevic reportedly signed a petition calling for peace and displayed banners reading "While one part of Serbia is screaming, another is singing"—a reference to the rock concerts held in Belgrade. In another incident, reservists who had been called up for duty and gathered at their mobilization point in Zabare suddenly declared that they did not want to go to Kosovo.[40] Several of Serbia's small, nonparliamentary parties offered their support to the organizers of the protests, "demanding that the authorities make more political concessions to end the war, initiate negotiations, and make it possible for the soldiers to return to their homes."[41]

The antiwar protests in these communities of south-central Serbia almost certainly proved of more than passing concern to the leaders in Belgrade in that they were occurring in the supposed heartland of the Serbian Socialist Party, an area where Milosevic had carried large majorities in past elections.[42]

BOMBING PROMPTED CALLS FROM PARTY LEADERS AND ELECTED OFFICIALS FOR A NEGOTIATED SETTLEMENT

Initially, the NATO bombing caused the leaders of Serbia's opposition parties to rally around the flag and support Serbia's defiance of

---

[38]Gall, May 25, 1999. See also, *V.I.P. Daily News Report 1512*, May 24, 1999.

[39]*V.I.P. Daily News Report 1515*, May 27, 1999, and *1518*, June 1, 1999.

[40]See Lindsay Hilsum (*London Observer*), "Serbs Protest Kosovo Fighting," *Washington Times*, May 24, 1999, p. A1.

[41]See "Two Months of Air Campaign Against Yugoslavia," May 27, 1999.

[42]Hilsum, May 24, 1999, p. A1.

the NATO ultimatum regarding Kosovo. For the Serbian opposition, any suggestion of support for NATO's war would have been political suicide. Furthermore, most opposition leaders shied away from criticizing the Milosevic government too strongly for fear of repression or even murder.[43]

The first sign of a crack in the political leadership's unity occurred on April 25, when Deputy Prime Minister Vuk Draskovic, who previously had supported Milosevic's policies on Kosovo, publicly urged the government to seek a compromise peace that would allow an armed U.N. force, including some NATO troops, to police a political settlement.[44] Draskovic, who as head of the Serbian Renewal Movement was once the main opposition leader,[45] called on state leaders in a television interview to "stop lying to the people in Serbia":

> The people should be told that NATO is not facing a breakdown, that Russia will not help Yugoslavia militarily and that the world public opinion is against us.[46]

In his interview, Draskovic insisted that Milosevic had "supported the general direction" of his statement.[47] But such support appeared problematic, as shortly after the interview, Milosevic established military control over the Renewal Movement's television station and fired Draskovic from the cabinet.[48]

---

[43]The April 11 assassination of the independent publisher Slavko Curuvija "further chilled political expression already limited by wartime censorship. Opposition journalists and politicians understood Mr. Curuvija's killing, after state media accused him of being unpatriotic, as a clear message to them all." Erlanger, May 21, 1999, p. A13.

[44]Steven Erlanger, "A Liberal Threatens Milosevic with Street Protests," *New York Times*, April 27, 1999, p. A13.

[45]After having mobilized nationwide street protests against Milosevic in 1996 and 1997, Draskovic joined the government in January 1999, contending that a unity government was needed to face the Kosovo crisis. Erlanger, May 21, 1999, p. A13.

[46]George Jahn, "Strikes Destroy Novi Sad's Last Bridge," *Washington Times*, April 26, 1999, p. A15.

[47]Erlanger, April 27, 1999, p. A13.

[48]Many of Draskovic's former supporters had come to see Draskovic as an opportunist and suspected that his break with the government was an attempt to distance himself from responsibility for an ugly and wearying war. Ibid.

In mid-May, the mayors of the Serbian towns of Nis and Cacak issued statements calling on Milosevic to negotiate a quick end to the war.[49] On May 18, the mayor of Cacak, an industrial town 100 miles to the south of Belgrade, organized a "citizens parliament" as "a forum for the people to express their ideas on stopping the bombing, saving the economy, and ensuring the return of refugees." Immediately after its formation, the mayor was forced into hiding. However, the "citizens parliament," made up primarily of intellectuals—lawyers and teachers—persisted, and its members sent an open letter to Milosevic calling on him to stop the war immediately. The group's weekly protests calling for a negotiated peace were eventually stopped by the police.[50]

Around the same time, additional national opposition leaders in Serbia began to openly urge the Milosevic regime to work harder to achieve a diplomatic solution to end NATO's air strikes. The head of the National Peasants Party, Dragan Veselinov, for example, stated: "We urge NATO to end the attacks, but we also think the Serbian government should come out of its bunker, where they have both electricity and water, and suggest new solutions for Kosovo's status in Serbia and Yugoslavia."[51]

Even the ultranationalist deputy prime minister of Serbia, Vojislav Seselj, eventually came around to admitting publicly that some concessions were necessary. On May 30, Seselj announced that while he still opposed NATO forces inside Serbia, he would now accept foreign forces in Kosovo. Seselj also signaled that he was now willing to accept a severely truncated Serb presence in Kosovo by indicating his approval of the Chernomyrdin "proposal to leave at least some Yugoslav security forces inside Kosovo to guard the borders and preserve the symbols of sovereignty."[52]

---

[49]Erlanger, May 21, 1999, p. A13.

[50]See Hilsum, May 24, 1999, pp. A1 and A11, and Gall, May 25, 1999, p. A17.

[51]Rowan Scarborough, "Bombing Utilities Could Backfire, Experts Warn," *Washington Times*, May 25, 1999, p. A14.

[52]Steven Erlanger, "Dozens of Civilians Are Killed As NATO Air Strikes Go Awry," *New York Times*, June 1, 1999, p. A12.

THE FINAL PEACE SETTLEMENT WAS MET WITH RELIEF

The public response in Serbia to the announcement of a peace settlement seemed uniformly positive. Journalists reported that the
residents of Belgrade and other Serbian population centers manifested relief that Milosevic had accepted a settlement for Kosovo that
would end the bombing.[53]

In the words of the Yugoslav Army's June 10 press release, the cessation of the NATO air raids was "met with relief throughout the
country":

> When the news was broadcast many people gathered in the streets
> to rejoice. People were singing, drove around the town honking,
> and even shots were heard as if it were New Year's or our national
> team [had] triumphed in some important international match.[54]

Even when the nature of Milosevic's concessions became more
widely known, there was no public outcry or demonstration against
the settlement's terms. Opposition leaders such as Vuk Draskovic,
while willing to attack Milosevic and his government on other
grounds, for the most part had only praise for the peace agreement.[55]
The major exception was the extreme nationalist Vojislav Seselj, who,
along with his Radical Party parliamentary faction, denounced and
voted against the agreement. However, the opposition of Seselj and
his colleagues was limited: He and his faction decided to remain
within the government and eschewed mounting a public protest
against the June 3 settlement.[56]

---

[53]Adrian Dascalu, "Agreement Brings Relief for Yugoslav Citizenry," *Washington Times*, June 4, 1999, p. A12, and Robert Block, "Struggle for Milosevic's Political Life Begins," *Wall Street Journal*, June 11, 1999, p. A16.

[54]See Yugoslav Army Supreme Command Headquarters—Information Service, Daily Review 68, "NATO Raids on Manufacturing and Civilian Facilities on June 9th and in the Night Between June 9th and 10th, 1999," Press Center, June 10, 1999.

[55]Robert Block, "Belgrade's Papers Are Filled with Broadsides Aimed at Milosevic in Wake of Kosovo Accord," *Wall Street Journal*, June 7, 1999, p. A14.

[56]Seselj at first threatened to withdraw from the Serbian government on the ground that he could not "accept the entrance of foreign troops from aggressor countries into Kosovo." But he quickly backed away from this pledge, declared he would remain in the government, and promised Milosevic that he would not attempt to pull down the government by voting against it in the parliament or "organize any demonstrations against the Kosovo deal in the streets." Seselj eventually agreed to join the federal

BOMBING MADE CONCESSIONS POLITICALLY FEASIBLE

The mounting calls for a political settlement that would end the NATO bombings apparently persuaded Milosevic that he would not suffer serious political consequences if he made significant concessions on Kosovo. As noted above, Milosevic's manner of governance was authoritarian rather than dictatorial, and he knew he would eventually have to rely on elections (and his ability to manipulate the ballot) to extend his rule. Concessions that would have been politically dangerous for Milosevic to accept in March could now be justified—even to the Serbian military and the extreme nationalists—as a necessary price to stop the bombing. Thus, in the end, the allies' assumption that bombing would provide Milosevic with the political cover to concede on Kosovo proved correct. However, the allies grossly misestimated the magnitude and duration of the bombing that would be needed to establish that political climate.

---

government as well, taking the seat vacated by Vuk Draskovic. See Steven Erlanger, "In Milosevic's Government, Resignation over Pact, Confidence in His Strength," *New York Times*, June 5, 1999, p. A5, and "Ignoring Scars, Milosevic Is Stubbornly Pressing On," *New York Times*, October 31, 1999, p. A1.

Chapter Six

DAMAGE TO "DUAL-USE" INFRASTRUCTURE
GENERATED GROWING PRESSURE

According to sources inside his government, Milosevic, by the beginning of June, was "under increasing internal pressure, especially from his closest associates, to compromise [so as] to halt the devastating bombing campaign."[1] One source "close" to the FRY government reported that by the second week of May members of Milosevic's inner circle had begun to "break into pro-war and antiwar camps," with the latter faction starting to lobby for war termination. Because Milosevic seemed determined to fight on, the "antiwar" faction focused its lobbying efforts on the president's wife and influential confidante, Mira. The lobbying, said the source, "gained momentum as the war continued," and eventually Milosevic was under "tremendous pressure from all sides: the West, the inner circle, and his wife."[2]

Much of the impulse for this pressure seems to have resulted from NATO attacks on six types of fixed infrastructure targets—command, control, and communication (C^3), electric power, industrial plant, leadership, LOCs, and POL facilities—the bulk of which were located

---

[1]Carla Anne Robbins, Tom Ricks, and Robert Block, "Envoys Start Kosovo Talks in Belgrade," *Wall Street Journal*, June 3, 1999, p. A21.

[2]The source told *Newsweek*, "I can't pinpoint an exact moment when Milosevic finally listened, but there was tremendous pressure from all sides: the West, the inner circle, and his wife. It was building up, and eventually he just let go." See "NATO's Game of Chicken," July 26, 1999, p. 61. NATO officials believed that the political and economic elite in Belgrade had started to grow unhappy with the war by late April. See Michael R. Gordon, "Kremlin Says NATO As Well As Serbs Must Compromise," *New York Times*, April 27, 1999, pp. A1 and A12.

in Serbia proper. The vast majority of these targets were of the "dual use" variety in that they served a civilian as well as a military function, and as previously mentioned, part of the rationale for attacking these targets was to cause the civilian population to bring pressure on the Belgrade government to terminate the conflict. Together, these six types of infrastructure targets accounted for about 55 percent of the 420 or so fixed targets that were struck during the course of the air campaign.[3] However, they accounted for fewer than 15 percent of the nearly 10,000 desired mean points of impact (DMPIs) that were hit.

The attacks on these targets generated a growing interest on the part of Milosevic and his associates to end the conflict because the air attacks (1) were causing a magnitude of damage to Serbia's infrastructure and economy that, if allowed to continue, might eventually threaten the regime's survival and (2) were creating stress, hardships, and costs for members of the ruling elite.

THE DAMAGE TO SERBIA'S INFRASTRUCTURE AND ECONOMY WAS BECOMING SEVERE

By the time Ahtisaari and Chernomyrdin met with Milosevic on June 2, NATO's air campaign had already caused major damage to the FRY's infrastructure and economy. The vast bulk of the damage was concentrated in Serbia, the area of transcending political importance to Milosevic and his colleagues.[4] By June 2, the infrastructure targets that had been destroyed or damaged in Serbia included:

---

[3]According to internal Air Force "fact sheets" reportedly based on the Air War over Serbia (AWOS) database, a total of 421 fixed targets were attacked during the NATO air campaign, including 106 ground force facilities, 88 C-4I facilities, 68 LOC sites (mainly road and railroad bridges), 60 integrated air defense (IAD) sites, 30 POL refineries and storage facilities, 17 industrial plants, 19 electric power facilities, 18 border posts, 8 airfields, and 7 "counter-regime" facilities. Some 35 percent of these 421 fixed targets were said to have been destroyed, roughly 10 percent apparently received no damage, and the remainder "received varying levels of damage from light to severe." See Arkin, June 13, 2000, p. 1.

[4]A moderate amount of this infrastructure damage occurred in Kosovo but very little in Montenegro, which for political reasons largely escaped NATO attack.

- Fifty highway and railroad bridges. The dropping of these bridges disrupted the movement of military and civilian traffic along many of Serbia's most important LOCs.[5]

- Two oil refineries and a substantial portion of Serbia's stored POL stocks. The two refineries, which constituted the FRY's entire refining capacity, were largely destroyed. NATO's initial damage assessment estimated that some 57 percent of the FRY's petroleum reserves were destroyed or significantly damaged, but this estimate may be too high, as some of the Serbian POL storage sites were apparently empty when struck, their contents having been drained and dispersed before the air attacks started.[6] To limit the importation of foreign POL into Serbia, NATO air strikes dropped the railroad bridges that connected the Montenegrin ports with Serbia and also dropped bridges that crossed the Danube, which restricted POL imports by barge along that river.[7] However, some oil was still entering the country as of late May.[8]

- Fourteen Serbian industrial facilities, including a number of "dual-use" factories owned by close associates of Milosevic.[9]

---

[5]The VJ Supreme Command reported that a total of 55 bridges in the FRY had been hit by June 6. In its initial damage assessment, NATO counted 11 of the railroad bridges and 34 highway bridges as having been destroyed or significantly damaged. See Yugoslav Army Supreme Command Headquarters—Information Service, "55 Bridges Demolished," Press Center, June 6, 1999, and U.S. Department of Defense, Report to Congress, *Kosovo/Operation Allied Force After-Action Report,* January 31, 2000, p. 82.

[6]The Jugopetrol oil depot at Bor, for example, was emptied and cleaned before it was struck by NATO aircraft. See United Nations Environment Programme (UNEP) and United Nations Centre for Human Settlements (UNCHS) Balkan Task Force, *BTF—Hot Spot Report Bor,* 1999, p. 2. See also U.S. Department of Defense, January 31, 2000, p. 82.

[7]See United States Energy Information Administration, "Serbia and Montenegro," June 1999, p. 2, http://www.eia.doe.gov/emeu/cabs/sermont.hmtl.

[8]Raymond Bonner, "Oil Flowing to Yugoslavia Despite NATO's Exertions," *New York Times,* May 25, 1999, p. A17.

[9]A listing of the factories struck can be found in Yugoslav Army Supreme Command Headquarters—Information Service, "Industrial or Manufacturing Facilities Demolished or Damaged by the NATO Aggression," Press Center, May 22, 1999, and United Nations Environment Programme (UNEP) and United Nations Centre for Human Settlements (UNCHS) Balkan Task Force, 1999, pp. 12–21.

- Nine of Serbia's major electric power–generating facilities and a number of Serbian electric power transmission towers. The attacks on electric power targets produced major power disruptions (some of protracted length) throughout Serbia, causing electrical blackouts and a lack of running water in many cities, towns, and villages. As a result of the May 22 attacks alone, some 70 percent of Serbia's power reportedly went down.[10]

The Bombing and Sanctions Were Devastating to an Already Diminished Economy

As the air campaign drew on, it became increasingly apparent to the Belgrade leadership that the NATO attacks on infrastructure targets were doing significant additional damage to a Serbian economy that was already in serious decline.[11] Estimates of the costs of repairing the physical destruction in Serbia ranged in the tens of billions of U.S. dollars, a daunting amount for a pariah government bereft of foreign current reserves and with virtually no prospect of receiving loans from international lending agencies.[12] According to some estimates, it was going to take Yugoslavia some 15 years just to recover to the economic level that existed prior to the start of the bombing.[13]

---

[10]Yugoslav Army Supreme Command Headquarters—Information Service, Daily Review 50, "NATO Raids on Manufacturing and Civilian Facilities on May 22nd and in the Night Between May 22nd and 23rd, 1999," Press Center, May 23, 1999. A "map to the electrical power outages in Yugoslavia" is presented in Headquarters United States Air Force, *Initial Report: The Air War over Serbia*, no date, p. 29. See also Arkin, "Smart Bombs, Dumb Targeting?" *Bulletin of the Atomic Scientists*, May/June 2000, p. 52.

[11]Not only had the economy been battered by years of sanctions, it had also suffered heavily from the trade dislocations that had resulted from the breakup of the former Yugoslavia and the continued vicissitudes of communist mismanagement. As the CIA analysis put it: "One singular factor in the economic situation of Serbia is the continuation in office of a communist government that is primarily interested in political and military mastery, not economic reform." Central Intelligence Agency, *The World Factbook 1998*, p. 414. See also Steven Erlanger, "Fruit of Miscalculation," *New York Times*, June 4, 1999, pp. A1 and A17.

[12]Estimates of the repair and replacement costs for the destroyed infrastructure in Serbia ranged between $20 billion and $100 billion. See Dimititrije Boarov and Christopher Bennett, "The Economic Cost of Mr. Milosevic," *Institute for War and Peace Reporting*, June 16, 1999, http://iwpr.vs4.cerbernet.co.uk/index.pl?archive/bcr/bcr_19990616_1_eng.txt.

[13]See Andrew Borowiec, "U.N. Sees Yugoslavia Taking Years to Recover," *Washington Times*, October 7, 2000, p. A7.

In addition to the damage caused by the air campaign, the Serb economy was also being squeezed by international embargoes and other sanctions. On April 26, the EU banned the sale of crude oil and petroleum products to the FRY. The EU sanctions also barred the provision of services or technology for targets that had been destroyed by NATO, and tightened restrictions on investments, and restricted export credits.[14] On May 1, 1999, the United States extended its own economic sanctions by requiring the licensing of all trade with the FRY and freezing asset transfers.[15] These sanctions effectively banned all U.S. trade with Serbia.

While the NATO allies failed to agree on a visit and search regime that would have allowed NATO ships to stop and inspect suspected carriers of contraband, the increased insurance rates caused by the war zone danger and the FRY's poor capacity to pay for its imports dissuaded many former suppliers from shipping fuel to Yugoslavia.[16] No POL deliveries were made to Montenegrin ports after May 1. However, smuggling allowed some POL to continue to flow into Serbia from neighboring countries.[17]

The Government Lacked Funds to Pay Pensioners and Troops. By June, the Belgrade government was so short of funds that it was unable to immediately pay the salaries of army reservists who had been called up for service during the conflict. Following the end of hostilities, returning soldiers in some areas set up roadblocks along LOCs to protest the lack of pay, and many soldiers eventually had to settle for only a portion of the wages actually due them.[18] Back in their hometowns, the reservists "faced a cruel reality—unpaid utility bills, overdrafts on their bank accounts, debts from family borrowing, no salary payments from their decimated employers and no jobs."[19]

---

[14]See United States Energy Information Administration, June 1999, pp. 1–2.

[15]See Thomas Pickering, Undersecretary of State for Political Affairs, Testimony Before the House International Relations Committee, May 13, 1999.

[16]Ibid.

[17]United States Energy Information Administration, June 1999, p. 2.

[18]While they were promised a wage of 700 German marks ($412) for each month of service in Kosovo, they actually received that same amount for their entire period of service.

[19]See "Rival Frustrations, *Institute for War and Peace Reporting,* July 13, 1999, http://iwpr.vs4.cerbernet.co.uk/index.pl?archive/bcr/bcr_19990713_3_eng.txt.

The government was also unable to pay pensioners the monies that were owed them. In lieu of cash, the pensioners, like some of the soldiers, were eventually issued "electricity, coal, and firewood coupons" for May and June.[20]

Concern That Serbia's Agricultural Harvest Might Be Endangered. Some Serbian agricultural experts worried that the shortage of fuel and the disruption of LOCs, combined with the other problems unrelated to the bombing that were plaguing their country's agricultural sector, might significantly reduce the availability of food for the Serbian market. After the NATO bombing began, farmers required coupons for fuel, but according to one report, "In April, they were entitled to 8 litres of fuel for each hectare; in May, only 4 litres. They say with so little fuel they can hardly reach their farms, let alone work on them." The experts feared that the fuel shortage, combined with blockages in transportation routes, might imperil the ability of Serbia's farmers to harvest their wheat crops and transport them to storage silos and processing plants.[21]

Unemployment Greatly Increased. The bombing created increased unemployment in Serbia, including that among the blue-collar workers who had traditionally tended to support Milosevic and his Socialist Party. One Belgrade economist estimated that NATO's air attacks had cost some 600,000 workers their jobs.[22] A senior columnist and editor in Belgrade, writing in the third week of May, put the number even higher, suggesting that as many as a million people had been forced to stop working on account of the bombing.

---

[20]See United Nations, Office for the Coordination of Humanitarian Affairs, Humanitarian Risk Analysis No. 4, Federal Republic of Yugoslavia, OCHA Belgrade, October 1, 1999, p. 5.

[21]See "Seeds of Discontent," *Institute for War and Peace Reporting,* May 25, 1999, http://iwpr.vs4.cerbernet.co.uk/index.pl?archive/bcr/bcr_19990525_2_eng.txt.

[22]The 600,000 included 100,000 workers whose companies had been destroyed in the air strikes and another 500,000 "cooperative employees" whose work depended on the output of the destroyed factories. An additional 600,000 workers were only "formally employed" because they were on "forced vacations" or recorded as "technological surplus." This 1.2 million unemployed, when added to the 853,000 persons already estimated to have been without work in January 1999, meant that the total number of unemployed in the FRY was around 2 million in June 1999. See N. Zivanovic, "Mirosinka Dinkic—An Economist Talks About Government Employment Programs: 'The Solution Is Not on the Farm,'" Belgrade *Blic,* June 7, 1999, *FBIS* translated text, FTS199906080001674.

He described a population verging on penury and suffering from an overriding feeling of "uselessness":

> It is almost impossible to work, much less get paid for it. According to official figures, more than half a million people have had to stop working—unofficially, the number may be twice as high. But few people actually go to a job. The "economy" effectively no longer exists. People are without money, and a monthly salary of 50 German Marks seems a dream. Pensions are being paid with a four month delay, and many people get by bartering goods, such as cooking oil, rice, sugar, bananas, and macaroni—all valued items in short supply. The price of cigarettes has doubled: a carton that used to sell for 10 German Marks before the war is now being offered for 20.[23]

The prevalence of conditions such as those described above posed the possibility of widespread future public unrest in Serbia. The ravaged country and economy, together with its joblessness, created "the sharp potential for internal strife or even a form of civil war," in the aftermath of the conflict.[24]

ATTACKS WERE PERCEIVED AS AIMED AT WEAKENING MILOSEVIC'S CONTROL MECHANISMS

A possible related concern of Milosevic and his colleagues was that the NATO air strikes appeared to be aimed at degrading the regime's instruments of control. The attacks on interior ministry buildings, command and control bunkers, intelligence facilities, and various MUP and military headquarters around the country were undoubtedly perceived as aimed at weakening Belgrade's control, as was the April 21 cruise missile strike on the 23-story USCE business center building in Belgrade that destroyed the offices of Milosevic's Serbian Socialist Party and that of his wife's Yugoslav United Left Party (JULL).

The attack on the high-rise office building also knocked three television stations off the air, including Radio Television Serbia (RTS), the

---

[23]See "National Unity: Utter Exhaustion," May 21, 1999.

[24]Erlanger, May 24, 1999, pp. A1 and A14.

government's major broadcast media outlet. During subsequent weeks, the leaders in Belgrade saw attacks on numerous other television and AM/FM radio transmission and relay facilities throughout the country, all aimed at degrading the regime's military C^3 and its capability to communicate with and mobilize support from its people.

Concomitant with these attempts to diminish Belgrade's capabilities to influence public opinion, NATO mounted a PSYOP campaign aimed at driving a wedge between Milosevic and the Serbian population. While stopping short of openly calling for the direct overthrow of Milosevic, allied PSYOP leaflets and radio broadcasts constantly emphasized Milosevic's responsibility for the continued conflict and implied that his removal was a way out for the Serbian people. One leaflet, for example, asked the Serbian reader:

> How long will you suffer for Milosevic? As long as Milosevic continues his program of destruction, rape, and murder throughout Kosovo-Metohija, Serbia will drift further into international isolation. Don't let Milosevic hold you hostage to his atrocities.[25]

While these attacks may have added to Milosevic's and his colleagues' concerns about the potential effects of future bombing on their safety and power should NATO's air attacks become extended, the destruction that had occurred by June 2 had not seriously eroded any of the regime's principal control mechanisms. Except for the death of the FRY air force deputy chief of staff, the regime's senior civilian and military leadership apparently emerged from the war intact.[26] Nor did the bombing of headquarters significantly degrade the capabilities of the MUP and the other FRY internal security elements, in part because many of these headquarters were undoubtedly empty of personnel when hit. Finally, even though great damage had been done to Serbia's broadcast infrastructure, suffi-

---

[25]See Joint Task Force Noble Anvil, *Psychological Operations Support to Allied Force*, July 14, 1999, p. 8.

[26]The FRY Air Force Deputy Chief of Staff, General Ljubisa Velickovic, was reported to have been killed "during an inspection of front-line troops." See "Kosovo Update," *New York Times*, June 2, 1999, p. A12.

cient television and radio facilities remained intact for the regime to broadcast its messages to the Serbian people.[27]

None of the antiwar demonstrations that occurred prior to June 2 posed a serious threat to the Belgrade regime—all were contained by local police forces. Even so, Milosevic and his colleagues had reason to fear that public unrest over the continuing war, while not yet sufficient to threaten his rule, might in time grow to a magnitude that could topple him from power.

THE BOMBING IMPOSED STRESS, HARDSHIPS, AND COSTS ON THE RULING ELITE

Besides threatening their hold on power, the bombing also imposed psychological and physical hardships on the ruling elite. As noted in Chapter 5, the NATO air attacks—whether against infrastructure or against other targets—caused severe stress for the average Serbian citizen. It seems likely that these attacks also adversely affected the lifestyle and psychological well-being of the families of Milosevic's governmental associates and business cronies and provided this elite with an incentive to push for an end to the bombing.

Persons close to the regime obviously did not suffer the shortages of fuel and consumer goods experienced by the average citizen. Indeed, during the bombing, one could still see "posh cars in Belgrade" and "encounter people who continued to live as if there had never been a war."[28] Even the most privileged elite, however, could not evade some of the vicissitudes of the bombing, such as the trauma caused by the frequent and prolonged air raid warnings. Members of this group probably also suffered in one way or another from the electric power blackouts.

By the beginning of June, Belgrade was receiving only about 6 percent of its normal power supply, and most of the city was also without water: When the electricity went down, the pumps providing

---

[27]By the conflict's end, no fewer than 17 out of the 19 RTS transmitters in Serbia had been destroyed. The cost of the damage inflicted on the media in Serbia was put at $1.1 billion. See "Minister: Damage Inflicted on Media Exceeds $1 Billion," BETA, May 30, 1999, *FBIS* translated text, FBIS19990530000788.

[28]See *V.I.P. Daily News Report 1525*, June 10, 1999, p. 6.

the water for drinking, bathing, and sewage became inoperative.[29] It seems highly unlikely that the extended families of all the persons connected to the regime were able to escape the effects of these citywide deprivations.[30]

The bombing was also destroying the assets of the ruling elite. The April 21 attack on the USCE building destroyed television stations owned by Milosevic family members, friends, and close political associates. Indeed, the raid was designed to send a clear message that the "alliance would now hit the business interests of Milosevic's family and friends."[31]

Milosevic may have also felt some concern about his own safety and that of his immediate family should the bombing continue. He no doubt considered the April 22 cruise missile attack on his official residence in Belgrade and the repeated NATO strikes during the latter part of May on the Dobanovci presidential villa and its associated command and control bunker as attempts at his assassination.[32]

Whether referring to these attacks or to other forms of pressure, CIA director George Tenet said in a June 11 speech: "We made Mr.

---

[29]See "Harsh Reality Under the Bombs," June 3, 1999. See also Yugoslav Army Supreme Command Headquarters—Information Service, Daily Review 59, "NATO Raids on Manufacturing Facilities on May 31st and in the Night Between May 31st and June 1st, 1999," Press Center, June 1, 1999.

[30]When the bombing ended, prominent members of the Serbian establishment were engaged in building private generators that would provide them with electricity in future power outages and digging private wells that would provide them with water if Belgrade were again faced with harsh water shortages. See *V.I.P. Daily News Report 1525*, June 10, 1999, p. 6.

[31]Steven Erlanger, "NATO Raids Send Notice to Milosevic: Businesses He Holds Are Fair Game," *New York Times*, April 22, 1999, p. A15.

[32]While Yugoslav officials described the attack on the Belgrade residence as "an assassination attempt," Pentagon spokesman Kenneth Bacon disagreed, describing the residence as a legitimate military target that included "security and military bunkers" and functioned as a "command and control bunker." According to Bacon, NATO's aim was to attack "the head of the military regime" so as "to cut that off and break the central nervous system" of the FRY military. See Michael Dobbs, "Allied Strike Denounced as 'Attempt on Milosevic,'" *Washington Post*, April 23, 1999, p. A33, and Bradley Graham, "Missiles Hit State TV, Residence of Milosevic," *Washington Post*, April 23, 1999, p. A33.

Milosevic's life pretty miserable in Serbia."[33]   However, given Milosevic's many options for avoiding air attacks—including displacement to safe houses in civilian residential areas—it is unlikely that the threat of death from bombing was a major factor in his eventual decision to come to terms.

The owners of the manufacturing facilities vulnerable to air strikes were undoubtedly among the most eager to get the bombing stopped. Indeed, part of NATO's purpose in attacking such factories was to prompt the "crony" owners of industrial facilities to pressure Milosevic to end the conflict.[34]   To spur such action, *Newsweek* reports that the United States conducted a "campaign of psychological coercion" that "targeted Milosevic's industrialist cronies by calling in or faxing warnings that their factories would be bombed within 24 hours."[35]

Other pressures were also brought to bear on Milosevic and his cronies. The members of the EU banned some 360 associates and close friends of the Yugoslav leader from entering and conducting business in their countries.[36] By early June, Western diplomats were reporting the "strong possibility" that the "massive" financial assets the associates and family members of Milosevic had stashed in Greece and in four Yugoslav banks operating on Cyprus would soon be frozen. Had they been imposed, such sanctions could have endangered at least some of the ill-gotten gains that Milosevic's family

---

[33]Bill Gertz, "Clinton Has Plans to Unseat Milosevic," *Washington Times*, June 30, 1999, p. A4.

[34]See Michael R. Gordon and Eric Schmitt, "Shift in Targets Let NATO Jets Tip the Balance," *New York Times*, June 5, 1999, p. A1, and William M. Arkin, "Smart Bombs, Dumb Targeting?" *Bulletin of the Atomic Scientists*, May/June 2000.

[35]"A source familiar with the operation" told *Newsweek* that "the Yugoslavs at the other end of the line were often unnerved, responding with such comments as 'How did you find me?'" See "NATO's Game of Chicken," July 26, 1999, p. 61.

[36]In May, Cypriot officials prevented Bogeljub Karic, a FRY minister without portfolio, and his wife from entering the island. Karic owned the Karic Banka, one of the principal "offshore banking units" that used Cyprus as a base but conducted business elsewhere. See Andrew Borowiec, "Milosevic Family and Cronies Have Billions Stashed Abroad," *Washington Times*, June 3, 1999, p. A10.

and cronies had accumulated from skimming public money and other proscribed activities during Milosevic's 12 years of rule.[37]

---

[37]According to some estimates, anywhere from hundreds of millions to several billion dollars of Belgrade's funds may have escaped international sanctions and been moved out of the country during Milosevic's rule. Following Milosevic's topple from power, Yugoslav central bank officials "accused the Milosevic regime of stealing more than $4 billion and siphoning it out of the country." Investigators believe that aside from members of the Milosevic family, some 200 crony "businessmen-politicians who controlled most of the nations state-run companies" were involved in the skimming. The Milosevic family reportedly owned a $6 million house in a posh suburb of Athens as well as a summer residence on the Greek island of Hydra. Marko Milosevic, the president's son, was such a conspicuous spender that the Greek Foreign Ministry was moved to put pressure on him to behave more discreetly when visiting Greece. Among Marko's more recent acquisitions was an Italian-made 80-foot motor yacht, reportedly priced at $3 million. See Borowiec, June 3, 1999, p. A10, Dusan Stojanovic, "Yugoslav Leader Rebuffs U.N. Tribunal Prosecutor," *Washington Times*, January 24, 2001, p. A11, and R. Jeffrey Smith, "The Hunt for Yugoslav Riches," *Washington Post*, March 11, 2001, pp. A1, A20, and A21.

Chapter Seven

DAMAGE TO MILITARY FORCES AND KLA "RESURGENCE" GENERATED LITTLE PRESSURE

Even though purely military targets were the primary focus of the NATO air campaign and accounted for the vast majority of the weapons expended, the destruction and damage to such targets probably did not generate the major pressure for war termination.

NATO'S OBJECTIVES IN ATTACKING MILITARY TARGETS

Some senior allied leaders considered the Serbian military establishment, particularly the Serbian ground forces deployed in Kosovo, to be Milosevic's key center of gravity. The destruction of these forces was seen as a means to:

- Deter and constrain the Serbian military from taking repressive action against the Kosovo Albanians.[1]

- Coerce Milosevic into complying with the demands of the international community, i.e., to accept the Rambouillet terms. While the potential consequences of a progressive destruction of Serbia's armed forces were not spelled out, the NATO leaders may have assumed that such an erosion would magnify Serb

---

[1]As former President Clinton described the objectives of the bombing that started on March 24, NATO aimed to "deter an even bloodier offensive against innocent civilians in Kosovo and, if necessary, to seriously damage the Serbian military's capacity to harm the people of Kosovo. In short, if President Milosevic will not make peace, we will limit his ability to make war." See Statement by President Clinton to the nation, March 24, 1999.

fears of an external invasion or prompt a coup from military leaders desirous of preserving their assets.

In the one consequence that was explicitly spelled out, allied officials specifically warned Milosevic and his military leaders that continued NATO attacks would eventually alter the balance of forces in Kosovo decisively against Belgrade's interests. Former Defense Secretary William S. Cohen and General Henry H. Shelton, chairman of the Joint Chiefs of Staff, told Congress on April 15 that NATO could effect the removal of Serb forces from Kosovo by degrading the Serbian military to the point where a "resurgent" KLA would have the "wherewithal" to start pushing the Serb forces out of Kosovo. General Shelton argued that the bombing could produce one of two outcomes:

> One is that Milosevic would decide that there's got to be a better way, i.e., that he would like to either start negotiating or settle with NATO; or until such time as the balance of power shifts between the uniform members of the Serbs and the KLA or UCK [Ushtria Clirimtare Kosoves, also known as Kosovo Liberation Army—KLA], that he sees his resources being diminished, his military being decimated or degraded to the point that the [KLA] is starting to have the wherewithal to move against him and to basically start pushing him out of Kosovo.[2]

The statement of General Wesley Clark, the supreme allied commander, Europe (SACEUR), on NATO's military mission embraced both the deterrent-constraint objective and the coercive objective:

> The military mission is to attack Yugoslav military and security forces and associated facilities with sufficient effect to degrade its capacity to continue repression of the civilian population and to deter its further military actions against his own people. We aim to put its military and security forces at risk. We are going to systematically and progressively attack, disrupt, degrade, devastate, and ultimately destroy these forces and their facilities and support, unless President Milosevic complies with the demands of the international

---

[2]Secretary Cohen and General Shelton presented their views in testimony before the Senate Armed Services Committee on April 15, 1999. See Bill Gertz, "Cohen, Shelton See Victory in Kosovo Without a Treaty: Bombing Can Reduce Enemy Power to That of KLA," *Washington Times*, April 16, 1999, p. A11.

community. In that respect, the operation will be as long and difficult as President Milosevic requires it to be.[3]

MUCH ABOVE-GROUND MILITARY INFRASTRUCTURE WAS DESTROYED

In their attempts to progressively degrade and destroy Yugoslav military and security forces, NATO attacked both fixed and mobile
("flex") military targets. The attacks on fixed, "purely" military targets were directed against ground force facilities (including barracks,
equipment depots, and ammunition storage sites), military C^3 facilities (including headquarters, subordinate command posts, and military communication facilities), air defense sites and related facilities
(including SAM sites, integrated air defense [IAD] sites, and airfields),
border posts, and military industrial facilities.[4] NATO's attacks on
mobile targets were concentrated on tanks, armored personnel carriers (APCs), and artillery in Kosovo.

The attacks on fixed targets destroyed or damaged much of the FRY's
military infrastructure, including the buildings housing its command
posts and headquarters, troops, equipment, and military repair and
production facilities, and its airfields and communication nodes.
Underground facilities and bunkers were also struck with effect
when they could be located and penetrated. According to prelimi-
nary bomb damage assessments (BDAs), these attacks are estimated
to have destroyed some 60 percent of the Third Army's physical infrastructure in Kosovo, 35 percent of the First Army's infrastructure
in Serbia, and 20 percent of the Second Army's infrastructure in
Montenegro.[5] Among other losses, the bombing destroyed an estimated 29 percent of the VJ's total ammunition storage capacity.[6]
About 50 percent of the FRY's modest defense industry was also es-

---

[3]Press conference by Secretary General Dr. Javier Solana and SACEUR General Wesley
Clark, March 25, 1999.

[4]Arkin, June 13, 2000, p. 1.

[5]Initial BDA estimates were presented in a June 10, 1999, Defense Department briefing
by Secretary of Defense William Cohen, General Hugh Shelton, and Lieutenant
General Charles Wald. See "Special Defense Department Briefing on Serb Withdrawal
from Kosovo and NATO Bombing Pause," *Federal News Service*, June 10, 1999.

[6]See U.S. Department of Defense, January 31, 2000, p. 82.

timated to have been damaged or destroyed, including 70 percent of its small aviation-related industry, 40 percent of its vehicle production, and 65 percent of its ammunition production.[7] Extensive damage was also done to some military stocks. These military infrastructure losses, like the "dual-use" losses, would be difficult for the cash-strapped government in Belgrade to replace. However, the effect of the losses on the FRY's war-fighting prowess was more long term than immediate.

THE SERBS ADOPTED COUNTERMEASURES TO REDUCE DAMAGE TO THEIR MILITARY STRUCTURE

Except for the FRY air force, which lost a significant percentage of its frontline MiG-21 and MiG-29 aircraft, the NATO attacks did not greatly diminish the FRY's combat structure. There are several reasons for this.

Most Fixed Targets Were Empty When Struck

The FRY military was well prepared for air attacks. Because the former Yugoslavia long considered the USSR its main threat, the FRY had built an infrastructure that was designed to withstand attacks from an enemy with vastly superior air power. To reduce the effects of air attacks, the FRY invested in numerous deep and hardened bunkers, dispersed storage sites, and redundant communication links that would prove difficult to identify and destroy. The FRY leaders also adopted contingency plans to remove troops and equipment from harm's way before any bombing began.

As a consequence, most of the purely military facilities that were struck by NATO aircraft and missiles were probably empty of personnel and equipment when they were hit. The long period of strategic warning that preceded the start of the air campaign gave the Serbs ample opportunity to vacate likely military targets and disperse military supplies and equipment. Postwar bomb damage inspections of C^3 facilities in Kosovo revealed "little or no equipment" in the purely military facilities that had been hit, suggesting that the

---

[7]"Special Defense Department Briefing," June 10, 1999.

facilities were not operational at the time of attack. However, the "dual-use" C^3 facilities that were struck appeared to have been "operational at the time of attack causing the destruction of most of the equipment along with the destruction of the buildings."[8] General Short believed that "all" the fixed military targets that NATO struck in Kosovo had been "evacuated long before" they were attacked. General Pavkovic, the Third Army commander, confirmed that evacuation was among the protective measures adopted by the VJ before the outbreak of hostilities: "We knew that [NATO] would try to make a good start by hitting our units, our command and control centers. So we undertook all necessary measures to protect our soldiers and equipment."[9]

A similar situation with respect to the evacuation of purely military targets also prevailed in Serbia. The First Army's infantry, armored, and artillery units had probably already dispersed to other areas when their barracks and other base facilities were struck. Many of the command centers and headquarters sites, such as buildings housing the General Staff and Federal Defense Ministry in Belgrade, were also emptied of their personnel and equipment.[10] Some of the depots holding VJ POL stocks and military support equipment were apparently emptied as well. It is also probable that the Serbs removed some of the equipment from the military industrial facilities that they considered to be priority targets for attack.

Only a Portion of the Structure Was Effectively Attacked

A second reason NATO did limited damage to the FRY combat structure was that only a portion of the ground force structure was

---

[8]See U.S. Department of Defense, January 31, 2000, p. 83.

[9]See Interviews with General Short, General Pavkovic, and President Ahtisaari, "Moral Combat: NATO at War," transcript of a BBC2 Special, March 12, 2000, pp. 24–25 and 32, http://news6.thdo.bbc.co.uk/hi/english/static/audio%5Fvideo/programmes/panorama/transcripts/transcript%5F112%5F03%5F00.bxt.

[10]The VJ bitterly protested the destruction of these "Belgrade landmarks," claiming that NATO knew that "these buildings were evacuated and practically stripped of their importance weeks ago, right after the first NATO air raids." See Yugoslav Army Supreme Command Headquarters—Information Service, Daily Review 28, "Statement by Colonel Milivoje Novkovic, Head of the Supreme Command HQ Information Service," Press Center, May 1, 1999.

actually attacked. NATO made no attempt to attack the dispersed infantry, armored, and artillery units of two of the FRY's three field armies: the First Army in Serbia or its Second Army in Montenegro.

Furthermore, those deployed force elements that NATO attempted to attack—the tanks, APCs, and artillery/mortars of the Third Army and the MUP in Kosovo—often proved difficult to kill because NATO "encountered significant difficulty in locating and positively identifying mobile ground targets."[11] The NATO air effort was hampered by a number of factors, including poor weather (cloud cover greater than 50 percent more than 70 percent of the time); the rugged mountainous and forested terrain in parts of Kosovo; the absence of a ground threat to make Serb forces concentrate and the style of small-unit warfare practiced by the Serb forces in Kosovo; the Serb use of dispersal, camouflage, dummy targets, concealment, and hardened bunkers and their exploitation of civilian populations and facilities as shields; the continued threat posed by Serbian air defenses; the tight ROEs that constrained allied air operations, including the requirement for "eyes on targets"; and the shortcomings in allied tactics and procedures for rapidly prosecuting attacks on fleeting targets.[12]

VJ ARMOR, ARTILLERY, AND TROOPS SURVIVED THE WAR LARGELY INTACT

The actual results of the air attacks on the Serb forces deployed in Kosovo are in dispute. A comprehensive NATO damage assessment conducted by a studies and analysis team at United States Air Forces in Europe (USAFE) concluded that allied aircraft had achieved "successful hits" on 93 tanks, 153 APCs, 389 artillery and mortar tubes, and 339 military vehicles in Kosovo. However, the assessment provided no data on the proportion of total mobile targets that were hit or "the level of damage inflicted on the targets that were struck."[13]

---

[11]See U.K. Ministry of Defence, *Kosovo: Lessons from the Crisis*, June 2000, Chapter 7, p. 9.

[12]For discussions of the effects of weather, camouflage, concealment, and deception in Kosovo, see U.S. Department of Defense, January 31, 2000, pp. 60–63, and U.K. Ministry of Defence, June 2000, Chapter 7, pp. 2 and 9.

[13]See U.S. Department of Defense, January 31, 2000, pp. 84–86.

The investigating teams that surveyed the Kosovo battlefield reportedly found the hulks of only 26 tanks (or, according to some sources, 14 tanks and 12 self-propelled artillery vehicles, "which looked like tanks"), 18 APCs, and 20 artillery pieces. All of these "catastrophic kills" had been abandoned in place by the Serbs.[14] The remaining 67 tanks, 135 APCs, and 369 artillery and mortar tubes that had been "successfully struck" were assumed to have been either repaired and returned to duty in Kosovo or transported back to Serbia for salvage and repair.[15] There was the further assumption that some of the equipment that had been damaged or destroyed was replaced by new equipment brought in from Serbia at night.

Critics contend that the methodology and evidence used for determining some of the "successful strikes" were suspect and that the amount of equipment actually damaged by the NATO air strikes was probably considerably less than claimed.[16] *Newsweek* cited a

---

[14]The on-site battlefield investigations were conducted by elements of a multiservice Munitions Effectiveness Assessment Team (MEAT) whose findings were fed into the more comprehensive NATO Kosovo Strike Assessment and the U.S. Air Force Air War over Serbia studies. The NATO assessment specified 26 catastrophic tank kills and, according to its briefing chart, "Final v. Initial Assessment," also seems to have endorsed the on-site MEAT investigating-team findings that 18 APCs and 20 artillery pieces were catastrophic kills. See Briefing and press conference on the Kosovo Strike Assessment by General Wesley K. Clark, Supreme Allied Commander, Europe, and Brigadier General John Corley, Chief, Kosovo Munitions Effectiveness Assessment Team, NATO Headquarters, September 16, 1999. See also John Barry and Evan Thomas, "The Kosovo Cover-Up," *Newsweek*, May 15, 2000, pp. 23–26, and Stephen P. Aubin, "*Newsweek* and the 14 Tanks," *Air Force Magazine*, July 2000.

[15]According to Brigadier General Corley, there was "extensive evidence" that the Serbs quickly removed damaged equipment from the battlefield, in part to mask the amount of damage being inflicted on their forces. He speculated that some of the vehicles that were "successfully struck" received damage that might have caused them to lose their mobility. "For example, the tread might have been knocked off of the tank. And it would be removed and then brought back into repair, not unlike we would have a car towed from the side of the highway into a repair shop or to have a flat repaired on the side of the road." In contrast, the abandoned equipment the investigating teams had found on the ground in Kosovo had received such "catastrophic damage" that it "would not have any future utility from a military perspective." See Briefing and press conference on the Kosovo Strike Assessment, September 16, 1999, and U.S. Department of Defense news briefing by Brigadier General John Corley, May 8, 2000.

[16]According to the methodology employed in the Kosovo Strike Assessment, the assessment of a successful strike on a target not found on site was based on a mission report plus at least one of the following corroborative sources of intelligence: cockpit video, poststrike imagery, prestrike imagery plus another valid intelligence source, a combination of two valid intelligence sources, Forward Air Controller (FAC) interview

November 1999 "get-together of U.S. and British intelligence experts, which determined that the Yugoslav Army after the war was only marginally smaller than it had been before."[17] Serb military sources also assert that their armored and artillery losses from the bombing were low.[18] A comparison of the FRY's declarations of its armored and artillery inventories as of January 1, 1999, and January 1, 2000, also reflected small losses. The January 1, 2000, declaration, which is subject to third-country audit under the Dayton Accords, showed a net reduction of 9 tanks, 39 APCs (including 19 APCs belonging to the MUP), and 28 artillery pieces.[19]

The actual intent of the damage inflicted by NATO air strikes on the VJ Third Army may never be precisely determined. Regardless of the eventual resolution of this debate, however, the conclusion of this analysis—namely, that attacks on fielded forces had little bearing on

---

confirmation, pilot-confirmed prestrike imagery, and witness. Of the strikes that were assessed as successful, some 55 percent were based on a mission report plus one other source, while some 45 percent were based on a mission report plus two or more additional sources. Critics of this methodology pointed to the heavy reliance on mission reports, a data source that had often proved unreliable in past conflicts, and to the use of confirmatory data that was sometimes less than persuasive. John Barry of *Newsweek* has alleged, for example, that among the 55 percent of strikes based on a mission report "backed by only a single datum point, just over four in 10 had as lone source a bomb flash picked up by IR [infrared] sensors on the DSP [Defense Support Program] satellite, which confirms only that the pilot dropped a bomb; in most cases, it says nothing about what, if anything, the bomb hit." For different views on the sources and methodology used in the Kosovo Strike Assessment, see Briefing and press conference on the Kosovo Strike Assessment, September 16, 1999; U.S. Department of Defense news briefing, May 8, 2000; Barry and Thomas, May 15, 2000; Aubin, July 2000; Letters to the editor from John Barry and Stephen P. Aubin, *Air Force Magazine*, August 2000.

[17]See Barry and Thomas, pp. 25–26.

[18]General Pavkovic, the Third Army Commander, claimed that the destroyed equipment in the Third Army and the Pristina Corps included 13 tanks (only 7 of which he claimed were destroyed by NATO aircraft), 6 APCs, 8 artillery pieces, and 19 antiaircraft guns. The validity of Pavkovic's statements about Serb losses has been undermined by his simultaneous, greatly exaggerated claims of NATO aircraft (34), helicopter (5), and cruise missile (52) losses. See Radio-Television Serbia broadcast by Lieutenant General Pavkovic, June 11, 1999, *FBIS* translated text, FTS19990611001741.

[19]The January 1, 2000, FRY declaration lists losses in frontline combat aircraft (11 MiG-29s, 30 MiG-21s) that generally match the losses claimed by NATO. See Federal Republic of Yugoslavia, Agreement on Sub-Regional Arms Control, Information on the Army of Yugoslavia, Annual Data Exchange, valid as of January 1, 1999, and Federal Republic of Yugoslavia, Information on Armaments Limited by the Agreement on Sub-Regional Arms Control in Federal Republic of Yugoslavia, entry into force January 1, 2000.

Milosevic's decision to accede to NATO's terms—stands. Even if one assumes that all the equipment assessed in the Kosovo Strike Assessment as having received a "successful hit" proved to be beyond repair, the amount of equipment lost to air attacks in Kosovo would still constitute only a small percentage of the FRY's total equipment inventory. Tank losses would have reduced the total FRY inventory by about 9 percent, APC losses by 15 percent, and artillery losses by 10 percent.[20]

FRY leaders claimed that their personnel losses in the conflict were also comparatively modest. According to Milosevic, only 462 members of the VJ and 114 members of the MUP were killed.[21] These numbers seem low given the size of the casualties some Serbian communities apparently suffered.[22] However, the personnel losses actually suffered were probably easily absorbed in a FRY military and police establishment that numbered more than 200,000.[23]

SERB FORCES IN KOSOVO WERE ABLE TO CARRY OUT MOST OF THEIR MISSIONS

Despite the losses and disruption caused by the bombing, leaders in Belgrade apparently continued to believe that the Serb forces in Kosovo remained capable of carrying out most of their key missions. This was clearly the view of General Pavkovic, the Third Army com-

---

[20]As of January 1, 1999, the FRY claimed a tank inventory of 1029, an APC inventory of 975, and an artillery inventory of 3922. These numbers include equipment assigned to the MUP as well as the VJ. See Federal Republic of Yugoslavia, January 1, 1999.

[21]General Pavkovic claimed that the Third Army saw 161 men killed and 299 wounded in NATO air strikes. Milosevic's figures may include troops and police lost both to NATO bombing and in battles with the KLA. See Radio-Television Serbia, June 11, 1999, and "Yugoslav President Slobodan Milosevic's Address to the Nation," Belgrade *Borba*, June 10, 1999, *FBIS* translated text, FTS19990610001656.

[22]According to official figures, disputed by many locals, Kraljevo (population 50,000) lost 41 of its men during the conflict and Leskovac (an even smaller town) lost 57. See "Shoot First, Live Longer," *Institute for War and Peace Reporting*, July 21, 1999, http://iwpr.vs4.cerbernet.co.uk/index.pl?archive/bcr/bcr_19990721_3_eng.txt.

[23]According to the OSCE, the VJ in total had approximately 85,000 to 114,000 personnel with a reserve force of possibly 200,000. The International Institute for Strategic Studies puts the FRY's total active armed forces at 108,700 with some 400,000 reserves. See OSCE, December 1999, Part II, Chapter 3, p. 1, and International Institute for Strategic Studies, *The Military Balance 1999–2000*, London: Oxford University Press, 1999, p. 102.

mander, who asserted immediately after the conflict that the Third Army had "fully preserved" its "war potential and ability to continue waging extensive combat actions in all conditions."[24] Pavkovic was reportedly most reluctant to see Serb forces withdrawn from Kosovo. Moreover, despite NATO's attempts to interdict the LOCs and communication nodes leading into Kosovo, Belgrade maintained the capability to both command and control and resupply its forces in Kosovo.

There also can be little question, however, that NATO air operations limited the potential combat effectiveness of the Third Army forces in Kosovo. The constant threat of air attack forced the VJ to avoid large-scale operations and to disperse its forces within Kosovo's villages and in the countryside, where they sought shelter in mountain revetments and hid among the tree lines.[25] Had VJ forces continued to adhere to this dispersed posture in the event of an invasion by NATO ground forces, they would have had little capability for an organized defense.

But this dispersed and buttoned-up posture did not prevent the VJ or the MUP from carrying out—albeit with some difficulty—their immediate missions of (1) conducting ethnic cleansing, (2) rooting out and suppressing KLA elements in Kosovo, (3) preventing the infiltration of KLA forces from Albania, and (4) strengthening Kosovo's physical defenses against invasion.

Serb Forces Continued Ethnic Cleansing to the End

NATO air attacks proved unable to deter or significantly degrade the VJ's and MUP's capacity to repress and expel the civilian population of Kosovo. The company-sized or smaller task forces that the VJ and the MUP employed in their ethnic cleansing operations were difficult to locate from the air and would have proved difficult to attack with-

---

[24]See "Gen. Pavkovic Threatens to Take Serb Army Back to Kosovo," Belgrade *Tanjug* in English, June 13, 1999, *FBIS* translated text, FTS19990613000629.

[25]See Headquarters United States Air Force, no date, p. 26; U.S. Department of Defense, January 31, 2000, pp. 86–87; and Briefing and press conference on the Kosovo Strike Assessment, September 16, 1999.

out risking Kosovo Albanian civilian casualties.[26] Because these small Serb units could not be deterred or stopped, ethnic cleansing continued throughout the course of the air campaign, albeit at a decreasing magnitude.[27] However, the decline in the rate of ethnic cleansing was largely attributable to the diminishing size of the population pool undergoing the "cleansing." As previously noted, an estimated 90 percent of the Kosovo Albanian population had been internally displaced or expelled from Kosovo by June 2. Furthermore, the Serbs probably did not attempt to displace all the Kosovo Albanians, as they wanted to keep some minimum number in their areas of operation as shields against a future ground invasion or unconstrained air attacks.[28]

Serb Forces Continued to Root Out and Suppress the KLA

Up to the moment of their withdrawal, the VJ and MUP forces in Kosovo demonstrated a continued capability to dominate the battlefield in Kosovo. The key reason was that the KLA elements the Serbs faced in Kosovo were substantially smaller than the VJ and MUP forces (which combined probably numbered between 55,000 and 65,000 men) and were, for the most part, lightly armed and poorly trained and led.[29] The vast majority of the KLA rank and file remained villagers armed with an individual weapon, typically an AK-

---

[26]Paramilitary units and armed civilians also participated in these ethnic cleansing operations. The task forces were sometimes supported by one or more artillery pieces, APCs, and tanks.

[27]During the period May 19 to June 2, 1999, an additional 58,000 Kosovo Albanians were driven from Kosovo. Some 50 percent of the ethnic cleansing had occurred during the first two weeks of the conflict. See OSCE, December 1999, Part I, Chapter 1, pp. 2–3.

[28]In his *Frontline* interview, General Pavkovic said the Serbs realized that "if all the Albanian people were to leave, we would have been totally exposed to NATO attacks from the air." See Interview with General Pavkovic, PBS *Frontline*, "War in Europe," February 22, 2000, http://www.pbs.org/wgbh/pages/frontline/shows/kosovo/interviews.

[29]Even though the KLA's top military leadership improved considerably in April 1999, when Agim Ceku—a professional officer with considerable previous combat experience in Croatia—became their military commander, the KLA had only a small core of well-trained personnel "with the knowledge to provide leadership and backbone" to their forces. See OSCE, December 1999, Part II, Chapter 3, p. 6.

47, and with "a very rudimentary idea of infantry tactics."[30] The KLA fighters were typically short of weapons and ammunition and found it increasingly difficult to obtain supplies from Albania during the conflict.[31]

When confronted by VJ and MUP forces in April and May 1999, the vast bulk of the 24,000 or so fighters the KLA claimed to have recruited to its movement either retreated into Albania or discarded their arms and sought anonymity among the refugees.[32] Other KLA fighters retreated into the countryside of Kosovo, where they continued to operate in small guerrilla units—often of ten or fewer fighters—mounting occasional sniper and other ambush attacks mainly on Serb forces traveling Kosovo's roads. By mid-May 1999, only an estimated 3000 to 5000 KLA fighters remained in Kosovo, many of whom were situated in enclaves in or near concentrations of internally displaced Kosovo Albanians.[33] Even if these dispersed KLA guerrilla elements had been able to coordinate their operations—which was not the case—they lacked the manpower and firepower to effectively contest Serb control in the province.

Serb Forces Were Able to Deny the KLA Deep Incursions into Kosovo

The VJ was also able to defeat the KLA's attempts to mount large-scale penetrations into Kosovo from its base areas in Albania. Elements of the 10,000 or so KLA fighters located in Albania attempted major penetrations at several points along the Kosovo-

---

[30]Some KLA elements, however, were equipped with heavier weaponry, including light antitank weapons, shoulder-fired SAMs, rocket-propelled grenades, and heavy machine guns. Some KLA fighters also had sniper rifles, antitank mines, and explosives. See OSCE, December 1999, Part II, Chapter 3, p. 6.

[31]The KLA tried to open a supply route through Bosnia, and although a number of trucks initially got through, the Serbian authorities managed to close this route down.

[32]See Zoran Kusovac, "Croat General to Lead KLA as Part of Reorganization," *Jane's Defence Weekly*, May 12, 1999. For an assessment of the KLA at the outbreak of the air campaign, see "The KLA: Braced to Defend and Control," *Jane's Intelligence Review*, April 1999.

[33]Pentagon sources put the number of KLA fighters at closer to 10,000. See Paul Watson, "Despite NATO Rhetoric, Rebels May Be Ultimate Beneficiaries of Air War," *Los Angeles Times*, May 12, 1999, and Kusovac, May 12, 1999.

Albania border. In one of its few successes, the KLA managed to capture the VJ border post at Kosare in mountainous northwestern Kosovo, which provided them a tenuous supply line into the province. However, subsequent KLA attempts to advance more deeply into Kosovo were contained by well-dug-in VJ units backed by armor and artillery. During the week to ten days immediately prior to the Serb withdrawal, KLA forces, after intense fighting, were able to make some inroads in the Junik area of northwestern Kosovo.[34]

The major KLA offensive (code-named Operation Arrow) launched in late May in the Mount Pastrik area of southwestern Kosovo met with little if any success. Even after heavy NATO bombing of suspected VJ defensive positions, KLA forces were able to penetrate only a few miles into Kosovo during two weeks of fighting. As the Pentagon spokesman, Kenneth H. Bacon, described the situation, "In Mount Pastrik, the KLA failed to make significant inroads. They're in Kosovo, but they're pinned down."[35]

A subsequent examination of the battlefield around Mount Pastrik, which had been subjected to heavy B-52 attacks, showed surprisingly little evidence of damage to VJ forces or equipment. Indeed, the oft-cited claims that increased KLA ground activity during late May and early June had caused the VJ forces to mass and thereby become lucrative targets for NATO air attack generally were proven to be unsubstantiated.

THE BOTTOM LINE CONCERNING ATTACKS ON PURELY MILITARY TARGETS

In sum, neither the limited losses in ground combat capability the FRY suffered from the NATO bombing nor the "resurgence" of KLA military capabilities that supposedly occurred in late May of 1999 appears to have significantly influenced Milosevic's decision to come

---

[34]See Ian Fisher, "Aided by NATO Bombing, Rebels Position Themselves to Become Kosovo's New Army," *New York Times*, June 9, 1999, p. A14.

[35]Ibid.

to terms.[36] The reporting that Milosevic received from his military commander in Kosovo apparently continued to be upbeat throughout the war. Moreover, Serb officials, when addressing the reasons for Belgrade's decision to yield, mention neither the attrition of the FRY's military forces nor the supposed deterioration of the military balance in Kosovo as major reasons for Belgrade's decision to yield.

---

[36]For analyses of the Kosovo conflict that attach greater importance to the KLA factor in Milosevic's decision to yield, see Daalder and O'Hanlon, 2000, pp. 151–153 and 202, and Judah, 2000, pp. 282–284.

Chapter Eight

HE EXPECTED UNCONSTRAINED BOMBING IF NATO'S TERMS WERE REJECTED

According to Milosevic's own testimony and the contemporary statement of senior FRY officials and close Milosevic associates, the key reason Milosevic agreed to accept the terms presented to him on June 2 was his fear of the bombing that would follow if he refused.

NATO'S TERMS WERE SEEN AS A RUSSIAN-BACKED ULTIMATUM

The document the Finnish president, Martti Ahtisaari, presented to Milosevic on June 2 departed radically from the settlement terms Milosevic and the Russian envoy, Viktor Chernomyrdin, had discussed at their May 27 meeting.[1] Indeed, as previously mentioned, the terms being presented included two key provisions that both the Serbs and the Russians had long opposed: (1) that an international security presence with NATO at its core and under unified (read NATO) command and control be deployed to Kosovo to implement the agreement, and (2) that "all" VJ, MUP, and other Serb security forces be withdrawn from the province.

---

[1] As of May 27, Milosevic was apparently still holding out for a UN-commanded force in Kosovo made up of troops from states not participating in the attacks on the FRY. Milosevic also wanted to retain a contingent of 15,000 FRY troops and 10,000 police officers in the province. These terms were apparently included in the "agreement" he negotiated with Chernomyrdin on May 27. See *V.I.P. Daily News Report 1517*, May 31, 1999, p. 1, and "Radical Leader Says Russian Plan Fits with Yugoslav Principles," Belgrade *Borba*, May 31, 1999, *FBIS* translated text, FTS19990531001432.

After reading the document containing NATO's terms to Milosevic and the other assembled Yugoslav officials, President Ahtisaari made four important additional points: (1) that the Russian envoy, Viktor Chernomyrdin, who was also sitting at the table, had agreed to the terms presented in the document, (2) that the document's terms were nonnegotiable, (3) that the terms were the "best" that would be offered, and (4) that if these terms were rejected, NATO's pounding of Yugoslavia would continue and the Serb leaders would find the next NATO offer to be "worse" from their "point of view."[2]

Chernomyrdin's endorsement of the nonnegotiable terms laid down by Ahtisaari reportedly had a profound effect on the Serb leadership. Milosevic and his colleagues apparently concluded that the allies, with Russia's acquiescence, had presented Serbia with an ultimatum and that NATO was poised to launch a "fierce" and unconstrained bombing campaign if its terms were rejected. They anticipated that the future NATO attacks would focus heavily on Belgrade and would generally prove far more destructive than the bombing they had experienced to date. Indeed, the Serb leaders apparently were convinced that NATO was prepared to demolish Serbia's entire infrastructure—including its remaining bridges, electric power facilities, telephone systems, and factories—and concluded that they had no choice but to accede to NATO's demands to forestall such unacceptable damage.

When explaining the decision to accept NATO's terms, Milosevic and other senior officials have consistently asserted that the primary reason was to avoid the destructive bombing that a failure to yield would have inevitably unleashed. After hearing NATO's terms at the June 2 meeting, Milosevic reportedly sought assurance that Belgrade's compliance would bring a halt to the bombing. He first asked Chernomyrdin and then asked Ahtisaari the same question: "Is

---

[2]See Ahtisaari's descriptions of his meeting with Milosevic in Interviews with General Short, General Pavkovic, and President Ahtisaari, March 12, 2000; his Bonn news conference of June 3, 1999, *New York Times*, June 4, 1999, p. A17; and Blaine Harden, "A Long Struggle That Led Serb Leaders to Back Down," *New York Times*, June 6, 1999, p. 1. According to Judah's account of the meeting, Ahtisaari "warned Milosevic that, unless he accepted, the bombers would step up their destruction of Serbia's infrastructure, including the telephone system." See Judah, 2000, p. 278.

this what I have to do to get the bombing stopped?" He received an affirmative answer from both envoys.[3]

When Milosevic met with the leaders of the various political parties on the night of June 2 to inform them of his decision to accept the plan presented to him earlier that day, he reportedly told them: "The main thing is, we have no choice . . . to reject the document means the destruction of our state and nation."[4]

During a recent interview, Milosevic explained why he had felt compelled to accept the agreement presented to him by Ahtisaari and Chernomyrdin on June 2 even though it "was far more unfavorable" than the one he had negotiated with Chernomyrdin at their last meeting a few days earlier. Milosevic said that had the Serbs rejected an agreement that had been endorsed by Russia—a reputed defender of Serb interests—they would have been dismissed as a people "with whom you cannot reason in any way," and NATO would have been able to use the rejection as a license to engage in "even more massive bombing" at the cost "of a great number of lives":[5]

> I think, though I shall not speculate, that had we rejected that joint proposal of Russia and the G8, that is, the G-7 plus Russia, then there would have been yet another change for the worse that would have placed yet another trump card into the hands of our enemies, because all the time Russia had the reputation of a power that defended our interests. They would then have freely been able to say: they have said no to Russia and the Russian proposal. That means this is a country and a people with whom you cannot reason in any way because, behold, they have not even accepted the Russian proposal, which without doubt would have been in their favour by definition, and these unreasonable people have not accepted this. Without doubt, even more massive bombing would have followed in retaliation, with the loss of a great number of lives.[6]

---

[3]Tyler Marshall and Richard Boudreaux, "How an Uneasy Alliance Prevailed," *Los Angeles Times*, June 6, 1999, p. A1.

[4]See Doder and Branson, 1999, p. 274.

[5]Interview with Slobodan Milosevic, Belgrade Palma Television, December 12, 2000, *FBIS* translated text, EUP20001214000131.

[6]Ibid.

Milosevic's cataclysmic view of the likely consequences of continued defiance was echoed by other Yugoslav officials knowledgeable about the reasons underlying the decision to accept NATO's terms. One official, described as "close" to Milosevic and his wife, Mirjana Markovic, told an American reporter on June 5 that the Serb leaders believed that a rejection of the NATO terms would have prompted the "carpet bombing" of Belgrade:

> But we knew that when the Russians came in with this plan, that was it. We knew it from the beginning. We knew that the carpet bombing of Belgrade would start the next day after we refused, so what was the choice? . . . The alternative to acceptance was not a humane one. We couldn't be reckless and risk elimination of the state, the army, and the people for the sake of rhetoric, and without any substantial support in the world.[7]

The FRY Third Army commander, General Pavkovic, painted a particularly dark picture of Serbia's fate if it rejected NATO's demands. In remarks to discontented army reservists in Vranje on July 14, 1999, General Pavkovic claimed that Russia had betrayed and sold out Serbia (1) by not standing firm on a compromise peace proposal worked out by the Serbs that would have permitted both a Serb and U.N. force presence in Kosovo, and (2) by telling Serbia it had to accept NATO's terms or risk certain destruction. According to General Pavkovic, after first accepting the compromise peace plan:

> the Russians then came back and said we had to accept the Western plan, that we had to take it or leave it. We were told that if we refused the plan, every city in Serbia would be razed to the ground. The bridges in Belgrade would be destroyed. The crops would all be burned. Everyone would die. Look at the Russians. They have not helped us.[8]

In an interview reported in the private Belgrade weekly tabloid, *Nedeljni Telegraf*, General Pavkovic expanded on the reason the Serbian leadership felt compelled to accept NATO's peace terms. While asserting that the FRY army could have stayed and defended

---

[7]Erlanger, June 5, 1999, p. A5.

[8]Chris Hedges, "Angry Serbs Hear a New Explanation: It's All Russia's Fault," *New York Times*, July 16, 1999, p. A9.

Kosovo, General Pavkovic said it could not do so "while allowing the rest of Serbia to be destroyed." He reported that after the accord was accepted by the parliament, there was a meeting between Milosevic and the Supreme Command staff to assess what should be done next. He stated that it was the "threats that could have been fatal to the people and the country" that persuaded all the senior leaders assembled that a withdrawal from Kosovo was necessary.[9]

General Pavkovic said the terms presented by Ahtisaari and Chernomyrdin had "put the leadership in a big dilemma: to accept the ultimatum and spare the people and Serbia from annihilation, or reject it." He described the consequences of rejection as follows:

> The accord that was offered and then accepted was conditional: either you accept it, or the attacks will be more fierce. They said literally: the remaining bridges will be destroyed, the infrastructure demolished, towns bombed, and the entire power industry, and so on. They threatened to raze Serbia to the ground. In my opinion, they would have left Kosovo alone in that phase. Their plan was retribution against the people of Serbia, which they could not have borne after all that had happened. If we had decided to remain and allow all that to happen to the state, no one would have forgiven us.[10]

General Pavkovic suggested that NATO may even have been contemplating a strike on Vinca, the research facility near Belgrade, which housed a cache of some 60 kg of highly enriched uranium:

> Can you imagine what would have happened had they struck Vinca, like they threatened? And we know that in Iraq they attacked nuclear and chemical facilities. So, they could have attacked a facility like that here too. In that event all of Belgrade would have had to be evacuated to a distance of 100 km further away. It has been di-

---

[9]The interview was conducted by Milos Antic on Mount Tara and was published in *Nedeljni Telegraf* on August 25, 1999. See Milos Antic, interview with General Nebojsa Pavkovic on Mount Tara, *Nedeljni Telegraf,* translated in *FBIS*, East Europe, Balkan States (Serbia, Kosovo), "Gen. Pavkovic Interviewed; Sees Army Return," August 26, 1999, FTS19990826000853.

[10]Antic, August 26, 1999.

vulged that Wesley Clark wanted to strike the center of Belgrade the first day.[11]

While admitting that the failure of the Russians to back the Serbs to the end was "very relevant" to Yugoslavia's decision to accept the June 2 deal, Foreign Minister Zivadin Jovanovic said that the main reason was to stave off further attacks on Serbia's civilian population:

> Hospitals were left without electricity . . . you can't even store vaccines and heal wounded people. Civilian structures were being targeted. It was a most inhumane war. They tried everything but nuclear weapons. . . . I think they were getting out of their minds. NATO commanders were seeking excuses to burn the country and commit further massive killings. So the government, considering that the document guaranteed the territorial integrity and sovereignty of Yugoslavia, the equality of all in Kosovo-Metohija, and the turning over of competencies from NATO to the UN, decided not to risk massive genocide by NATO against the whole population. It was also fair to conclude that we would preserve our defensive capacity and so the government and leadership opted to accept the deal based on sovereignty and territorial integrity, the guarantee of a political solution based on autonomy and resolving of problems by the rules of the UN rather than NATO force.[12]

It is possible that both General Pavkovic and Foreign Minister Jovanovic resorted to deliberate hyperbole in describing the extent of the damage (e.g., widespread fallout from attacks on uranium stocks and "massive genocide . . . against the whole population") they believed would actually flow from any future bombing. Once the decision to yield had been made, the Serb leaders had reason to make a strong case justifying their action. However, this does not gainsay the evidence that Milosevic and the other Serb leaders believed they had been presented with an ultimatum on June 2 and that they expected something akin to unconstrained bombing if they rejected NATO's terms.

---

[11]Antic, August 26, 1999. The author is unaware of any evidence that NATO ever contemplated a strike on the Serb research facility at Vinca.

[12]Quoted in Judah, 2000, pp. 281–282.

WHY SERBIA'S LEADERSHIP FOUND THE THREAT OF UNCONSTRAINED BOMBING CREDIBLE

The question naturally arises as to how Belgrade officials could have so badly misread NATO's intentions and freedom of action that they would give credence to future air attacks as indiscriminate and destructive as those described above. The question is particularly salient given that the NATO commanders perceived their air operations to be tightly constrained so as to minimize civilian casualties and collateral damage.

As discussed above, Milosevic said he believed that a Serb rejection of peace terms endorsed by Russia would provide NATO with the license to engage in "even more massive bombing." There were probably five other reasons the Serb leadership found the threat of unconstrained bombing credible. These were: (1) the escalating pattern of NATO air attacks, (2) the evidence that NATO was postured for a greatly expanded air campaign, (3) the fact that NATO leaders had warned of devastating attacks, (4) the (mistaken) conviction that NATO was already purposely attacking civilian targets, and (5) the fact that Chernomyrdin was predicting massive devastation if the bombing continued.

NATO's Air Attacks Were Escalating

During the weeks preceding the June 2 meeting, Serb leaders had seen a major escalation in both the tempo and the targets of NATO air strikes. Around May 1, NATO aircraft were flying an average of 150 strike sorties per day. By the end of the month, strike sorties were averaging in excess of 250 sorties per day.[13] The number of strike sorties flown on the three days immediately prior to the June 2 meeting were 309 on May 30, 323 on May 31, and 319 on June 1.[14]

Attacks on "dual-use" infrastructure targets in Serbia also began to accelerate after May 1, when the NAC approved an expanded target

---

[13]See "Special Defense Department Briefing on Serb Withdrawal from Kosovo and NATO Bombing Pause," June 10, 1999.

[14]See NATO Headquarters, *Operation Allied Force Updates*, May 30–May 31, 1999, and Craig R. Whitney, "NATO Presses Attack, and Plans for Peace," *New York Times*, June 2, 1999, p. A13.

set and infrastructure targets became "more readily approved and systematically targeted."[15] The escalation was most notable in the attacks on Serbia's electric power grid. On May 2, NATO aircraft started attacking Serbian transformer stations with highly conductive filaments designed to short-circuit live electric power lines. While such attacks caused much of the central Serbian power system to shut down, the effects were only temporary. On May 22, NATO aircraft, using laser-guided bombs, switched to more lasting, "hard-kill" attacks on the Serbian power grid.[16] Attacks on key Serbian infrastructure targets continued to escalate during the period immediately preceding Ahtisaari's and Chernomyrdin's meeting with Milosevic. Between May 22 and June 2, NATO aircraft and missiles struck no fewer than 15 Serbian electric power transformer yards, 20 bridges and tunnels, 55 television and radio transmission and relay facilities, 20 POL storage sites, and 12 headquarters and command posts.[17]

The Serb leaders were acutely aware of the escalating nature of the allied air offensive. The VJ Supreme Command Headquarters, reporting on air strikes conducted on May 30 and the night of May 31, complained that

> [the] NATO air-force, intensifying its attacks from day to day, targeted numerous townships in the central part of the country. The aggressor continues to destroy the power grid, road and rail infrastructure, telecommunication systems, agricultural resources, residential areas in the towns and suburbs. All this is being done systematically and uninterruptedly for 69 days with the clear intent to aggravate the humanitarian catastrophe to an intolerable level.[18]

---

[15]See Headquarters United States Air Force, no date.

[16]See Arkin, May/June 2000, pp. 51–52.

[17]See NATO Headquarters, Operation Allied Force Updates, May 22–June 2, 1999.

[18]See Yugoslav Army Supreme Command Headquarters—Information Service, *Daily Review 58*, "NATO Raids on Manufacturing and Civilian Facilities on May 30th and in the Night Between May 30th and 31st, 1999," Press Center, May 31, 1999.

NATO Was Postured for an Expanded Bombing Campaign

Furthermore, as the weather for bombing improved with the approach of summer, the Serb leaders saw evidence that NATO was preparing for a greatly expanded air campaign. The number of NATO strike aircraft in the region had continued to increase and now numbered 535 aircraft, a force 250 percent larger than the force of 214 strike aircraft available at the start of the air campaign. NATO had also acquired additional bases in neighboring countries, including bases in Hungary and Turkey, that made it possible for its aircraft to attack Yugoslavia 24 hours a day from any direction.[19] The number of strike and supporting aircraft in the region would have allowed NATO to generate some 1000 attack sorties a day, a level of effort 300 percent greater than the level being flown in the days immediately prior to the June 2 meeting.[20]

The Serb leaders in Belgrade were surely aware of the general dimensions of the NATO buildup in strike aircraft and the threats of intensified attacks. The state-run paper *Politika*, for example, published a report from its correspondent in New York on May 31 detailing the deployment of additional U.S. aircraft to the region and citing a statement from a Pentagon spokesman that "we are intending to further intensify our air campaign."[21] The *Politika* correspondent went on to claim that U.S. newspapers were reporting "that, with the intensifying 'air campaign,'" American civilian leaders "have increas-

---

[19]Of the 535 strike aircraft, 323 were U.S. aircraft and 212 were aircraft of other NATO allies. By the end of the conflict, NATO aircraft were flying from bases in 15 different countries. See "Special Defense Department Briefing on Serb Withdrawal from Kosovo and NATO Bombing Pause," June 10, 1999, and Headquarters United States Air Force, no date, p. 25.

[20]The reason such a high level of effort had never been flown was that the number of available attack sorties significantly exceeded the limited number of targets that had been approved for attack. As Brigadier General Randall C. Gelwix put it, "We had a playbook of 900 plays, but were only allowed to use 50 of them." General Gelwix was deputy commander, 16th Air Force, and director, Combined Air Operations Center, NATO, Vicenza, Italy. See Headquarters United States Air Force, no date, p. 26.

[21]The *Politika* correspondent reported that 36 "F-15, 12 F-16, and 20 tanker aircraft had been sent to the region, bringing the number of U.S. aircraft participating in the murdering NATO fleet—which has 1,100 aircraft—to 769." See Darko Ribnikar, "Washington Is Opposing Peace," *Politika*, May 31, 1999, *FBIS* translated text, FTS19990601000520.

ingly placed the country's military leadership in charge of the military operations [in the Balkans]."[22]

NATO Leaders Had Warned of Devastating Attacks

The buildup of strike capability was accompanied by recurrent threats of more "intensified bombing" from various NATO spokesmen and by even more menacing statements from some NATO leaders, such as General Klaus Naumann of Germany, who observed that Milosevic was running the risk "that his entire country would be bombed into rubble."[23]

Serb leaders may also have recalled the warning that Lieutenant General Michael Short, the future air component commander of Operation Allied Force, had voiced in October 1998 to the commander of the VJ air force about the disfiguring damage that would be inflicted on Belgrade if NATO resorted to bombing:

> You've studied the Gulf war and the 1995 campaign in Bosnia. I know you believe you understand how I'm going to do my business. But you're not even close. No matter what you've done, you can't imagine what it's going to be like. The speed and the violence and the lethality and the destruction that is going to occur is beyond anything that you can imagine. If, indeed, you're not going to accept my terms, we need to break this meeting right now. I suggest you go outside, get in your car and ride around the city of Belgrade. Remember it the way it is today. If you force me to go to war against you, Belgrade will never look that way again—never in your lifetime, or your children's lifetime. Belgrade and your country will be destroyed if you force me to go to war.[24]

---

[22]Ribnikar, May 31, 1999.

[23]See Craig R. Whitney, "Confident in Their Bombs, Allies Still Plan for Winter," *New York Times*, May 5, 1999, p. A9, and Whitney, June 2, 1999, p. A13.

[24]When asked by the VJ general if he "really" meant what he said, General Short responded, "Absolutely. This is past the point of bluffing, and professional soldiers don't bluff." Interview with Lieutenant General Michael C. Short, PBS *Frontline*, "War in Europe," February 22, 2000, http://www.pbs.org/wgbh/pages/frontline/shows/kosovo/interviews.

NATO Had Already Attacked Nonmilitary Targets

The Belgrade leaders also found the threat of unconstrained future bombing to be credible because they believed NATO had already demonstrated a willingness to attack civilian targets. They were reinforced in this view by two perceptions.

First, the Serbs believed that many of the "dual-use" infrastructure targets that NATO classified as legitimate military targets, such as bridges, steam heat plants, and electric power facilities, were in actuality civilian targets. In keeping with their propensity to view themselves as martyrs, the Serbs saw the attacks on such targets as a form of "collective punishment" that NATO was exacting on the Serbian population as a whole.[25] They also saw the NATO attacks as purposely designed to create a "humanitarian catastrophe" and "deteriorate the living conditions of the population" to the point where their will to resist would be weakened.[26]

Second, many Serbs also apparently believed that NATO's bombing errors were not errors at all but deliberate attacks on civilian targets, again intended to demoralize and terrorize the public. The Serbs credited NATO with possessing sufficient intelligence, target identifi-

---

[25]As the independent Belgrade news agency BETA put it in a May 27 commentary:

> The attacks on the electric power systems have led ordinary people in Serbia to believe something repeated many times by the authorities, that the aim of the air raids on Yugoslavia was not to protect persecuted Albanians, but rather to dish out collective punishment and lead to the surrender of the country. At the same time, the alliance's extended list of targets and its readiness to continue the bombing at the same pace in the next two months, have only intensified such feelings. The pro-regime media have tried hard to convince the people that resistance to the bombing grows in NATO countries and that Russia and China will help Yugoslavia after all. To tell the truth, these claims have gradually become meaningless. Serbia's people are becoming aware that they are between a hammer and an anvil, and that the entire society is facing the danger of total destruction.

See "Two Months of Air Campaign Against Yugoslavia," May 27, 1999.

[26]See, for example, Yugoslav Army Supreme Command Headquarters—Information Service, *Daily Review 49*, "NATO Raids on Manufacturing and Civilian Facilities on May 21st and in the Night Between May 21st and 22nd, 1999," Press Center, May 22, 1999; *Daily Review 54*, "NATO Raids on Civilian and Manufacturing Facilities on May 26th and in the Night Between May 26th and 27th, 1999," Press Center, May 27, 1999; and *Daily Review 59*, June 1, 1999.

cation, and precision strike capabilities to rule out the possibility of bombing errors. Claiming that the "alleged" mistakes made by NATO pilots had been deliberate, General Pavkovic said:

> There were no mistakes, they have such technology that they could have hit even the smallest targets. Air strikes on civilian targets—Surdulica, Aleksinac, then trains, trucks, and buses, were not mistakes, but deliberate [actions], because they simply wanted to commit genocide against the Serbian people.[27]

The NATO attack on the Chinese Embassy in Belgrade on the night of May 7 had a particularly ominous portent for the Serbs. Virtually every Belgrader interviewed by one Western correspondent seemed convinced that the United States had intended to hit the embassy. The strike rattled many people, who saw it as a "sign that anything is a target." According to one Belgrader, the United States:

> did it on purpose to show the whole world that they are the only remaining superpower. To say to us: "How can such a small power [as Serbia] do anything, when the U.S. can do this to China."[28]

Chernomyrdin Was Predicting Massive Devastation If the War Continued

A final reason unconstrained bombing seems credible was that it accorded with what Viktor Chernomyrdin was telling Milosevic about the likely consequences of a failure to reach a settlement. In a post-conflict interview, Chernomyrdin revealed that during his several eight- to nine-hour meetings with Milosevic he explained to the FRY president why he was wrong to believe he would win the war and what would happen if he persisted in holding out, including "what would be left" of Yugoslavia if he attempted to do so.[29]

---

[27]See "Gen. Pavkovic Threatens to Take Serb Army Back to Kosovo," June 13, 1999.

[28]Belgrader Zoran Arsic, went on to say that he was sure the latest bombing signaled NATO's new determination to attack the civilian population: "Now they are going to bomb by day to scare the people." See Carlotta Gall, "Embassy Attack Followed by Defiance Toward NATO," *New York Times*, May 10, 1999, p. A10.

[29]Chernomyrdin described some of the meetings as stormy: "Can you imagine how uneasy was the discussion for 8, 9 hours? He would jump up, tear the papers, thrust

There is reason to believe that Chernomyrdin painted a bleak picture of "what would be left" if the air attacks continued.   As Chernomyrdin described it to one interviewer, "Ultimately, [all the parties] realized that the slaughter and the destruction of an entire sovereign country was in nobody's interest."[30] In his May 27, 1999, op-ed piece, published by the *Washington Post*, Chernomyrdin depicted the devastation that would be rendered by future bombing on Yugoslavia in terms similar to the cataclysmic images used by General Pavkovic and other Serb leaders:

> Now that raids against military targets have evidently proven pointless, NATO's armed force has moved to massive destruction of civilian infrastructure—in particular, electric transmission lines, water pipes, and factories. Are thousands of innocent people to be killed because of one man's blunders? Is an entire country to be razed? . . . More bombing makes it pointless to plan a return of refugees. What will they come back to—homes in debris, without electricity or water? Where will they find jobs, with half of all factories in ruins and the other half doomed to be bombed in due course? It is time for NATO countries to realize that more air raids will lead to a dead end.[31]

MILOSEVIC FEARED UNCONSTRAINED BOMBING MIGHT ENDANGER HIS RULE

Milosevic had every reason to contemplate with trepidation the prospect of unconstrained bombing. He realized that the FRY was now essentially isolated both militarily and diplomatically, surrounded by neighboring countries that had granted bases or overflight rights to NATO, and confronted by NATO settlement terms that had been endorsed by Moscow. He further recognized that Serbia had no defense against air attacks on fixed targets and that the weather for bombing was improving.

---

them, go out and come back again.   It was hard."   See Interview with Viktor Chernomyrdin, February 22, 2000.

[30]See Stabile, June 11, 1999.

[31]See Viktor Chernomyrdin, "Impossible to Talk Peace with Bombs Falling," *Washington Post*, May 27, 1999, p. A39.

Winter Would Magnify the Hardships of Bombing, Particularly Electricity Outages

Milosevic further knew that if there were no reconstitution or containment of the damage being inflicted on Serbia, the coming winter would greatly magnify the hardships of the Serbian people. In this respect, the prospect of a prolonged NATO denial of electric power was undoubtedly the most worrisome contingency, as it would severely affect the most basic needs of the citizenry.

- **Heating.** Widespread electricity outages could threaten the heating of 75 percent of the homes in the FRY.[32] The impact of a heating shortage of this scale would be extremely severe given that Yugoslav winters are very cold (below freezing temperatures for 63 days on average, and with temperatures sometimes below 10 degrees Celsius), Yugoslav homes are generally poorly insulated, and a large proportion of the urban buildings in Yugoslavia have no chimneys or alternative heating sources.[33]

- **Water Supply and Sewage.** As the NATO attacks on the power grid had already demonstrated, widespread electricity outages would also shut down Yugoslavia's water supply systems, all of which depend on electricity to power processing plants, control systems, and pumping stations. Wastewater plants would also be unable to operate properly during power outages.[34]

- **Food Storage, Preparation, and Processing.** Electricity outages would prevent the use of the deep freezers on which more than 50 percent of Yugoslavs typically depend for food storage.[35] Outages would also seriously hamper the cooking of food, "as practically all houses use electric stoves, as do most businesses

---

[32]According to a study prepared for the United Nations, electricity heats around 50 percent of FRY homes directly, while an additional 25 percent of homes rely on district/central heating plants that require electricity to pump water. See Colenco Power Engineering Ltd., "Electricity and Heating in the Federal Republic of Yugoslavia," U.N. Office for the Coordination of Humanitarian Affairs, Belgrade, September 20, 1999, p. 7.

[33]Ibid.

[34]Ibid.

[35]People typically purchase large quantities of food in the summer and autumn and store it for the winter. Op. cit., p. 8.

(such as bakeries) that produce cooked food."[36]   Much of the food processing industry would also be shut down by widespread electricity outages.

Milosevic Calculated He Could Best Survive in Power If Serbia Was at Least Partially Stable and Functioning

Milosevic apparently doubted that the Serb public would have passively accepted the severe hardships described above for long once the frigid Balkan winter set in.   He almost certainly realized that subjecting Serbia to further months of unconstrained bombing risked his continued hold on power.[37]   Moreover, with Russia's defection, it was highly unlikely that holding out longer would bring better terms.   This view was shared by his close aides, who reportedly found the courage to tell Milosevic that he should not reject the deal "only to accept a worse one later."[38]

---

[36]Ibid.

[37]Milosevic's sensitivity to the potential political consequences for his regime of the damage caused by the NATO bombing of Serbia's "dual use" infrastructure was manifested in the high priority given to the reconstruction of portions of that infrastructure after the war.   The reconstruction of bridges, for example, was conducted at a "frenzied" pace, with half the bridges destroyed or damaged in the bombing reportedly having been repaired by February 2000.   Media coverage of the reconstruction was fulsome, with state television almost daily broadcasting pictures of "construction workers promising to meet deadlines and government officials attending bridge-opening ceremonies."   (See Milenko Vasovic, "Serbia's Incredible Reconstruction," *Institute for War and Peace Reporting*, February 11, 2000, http://iwpr.vs4.cerbernet.co.uk/index.pl?archive/bcr/bcr_20000211_4_eng.txt.)

Ironically, one of the key reasons Milosevic is said to have miscalculated his chances for reelection in September 2000 was that his top aides gave him an overly "rosy picture" of the country's economic recovery.   Shortly before calling the election, Milosevic was being erroneously reassured that the "citizens were experiencing few shortages and that reconstruction of bridges, roads and factories damaged in NATO's 1999 bombing campaign was going well."   Milosevic rejected warnings that he was being deceived about the true state of the economy and the public's attitude toward him.   When the Socialist Party vice president, Zoran Lilic, advised him that "his position was very, very bad" and that any election would be "an adventure," Milosevic responded by saying that such fears were "not supported by any argument" and that the people appreciated "the patriotic reconstruction of the country."   See Smith and Finn, October 15, 2000, p. A30.

[38]Erlanger, October 31, 1999, p. A1.

Describing the calculations that led Milosevic to come to terms, Serb officials emphasized that "there was no longer any reason to wait." To continue the unequal war would be "pointless," they said, and would "obviously pose greater risks" to Milosevic's hold on power.[39]

Ljubisa Ristic, president of the JULL party and a close associate of the Milosevics, said it was obvious that NATO's final offer, which had been negotiated with the Russians, "had to be taken." Pointing to the fact that Serbia's air defenses could not shoot down NATO aircraft, Ristic said it was the last moment to save Belgrade and its population "from a more permanent loss of bridges, electricity, and infrastructure." Ristic also acknowledged that "it was the best moment for Milosevic and the regime to save themselves."[40]

This view was echoed by an independent Belgrade news analyst on June 4:

> This time around, Milosevic did not have much choice. He could have continued the war, which would result in the complete destruction of the country and enormous casualties as well as his probable overthrow at the end of the campaign. Instead, he decided to accept the peace plan, giving himself a little more maneuvering space in a bid to present his defeat as victory and to remain in power, together with his cronies, as long as possible.[41]

The private Belgrade news agency BETA, in its commentary of June 9, 1999, reported that the government "was faced with a choice to either continue to resist and risk a complete destruction of the country's infrastructure, or to accept NATO's demands." BETA went on to say that Milosevic, being a pragmatist, decided "to salvage what could be salvaged, that being his power in Serbia." It also suggested that the International War Crimes Tribunal's indictment of Milosevic on May 27 gave the FRY president an important additional incentive to stop the bombing in that he realized he could best postpone an

---

[39]See Erlanger, June 5, 1999, p. A5.

[40]Ristic's views were summarized in Erlanger, October 31, 1999, p. A1.

[41]See *V.I.P. Daily News Report 1521*, June 4, 1999, p. 5.

appearance before the tribunal in Hague only if he preserved at least a partially stable country in which his word remained decisive.[42]

---

[42]"Kosovo and Politics in FRY—A New Round Starts," BETA Commentary, June 9, 1999. *FBIS-EEU*-1999-0609.

Chapter Nine

HE PROBABLY ALSO WORRIED ABOUT THREAT OF
FUTURE INVASION

Concern about the threat that a future NATO invasion might pose for his regime was probably an added factor in Milosevic's decision to come to terms.

Serb military leaders from the outset had been sensitive to the possibility that NATO might eventually attempt to invade the FRY at one or more points along its borders. Once hostilities with NATO appeared likely, VJ forces began to take precautionary measures against such a contingency. Defensive positions were established and strengthened along possible invasion routes, particularly along the routes leading into Kosovo from Albania and Macedonia. The buildup of defenses started at the borders and then moved deeper into Kosovo.[1] Among other measures, some 80,000 mines were apparently positioned along Kosovo's border with Albania.[2]

Yeltsin discloses in his memoirs that Milosevic at one point said he would welcome a NATO invasion:

> He believed that the Yugoslav army was prepared to fight, and that the Yugoslav people were prepared to unite around Milosevic. At times, Milosevic even asked Chernomyrdin to conduct the negotiations in such a way that the ground operations would start faster.

---

[1] OSCE, December 1999, Chapter 3, p. 9.

[2] See AFP (North European Service), "Gen Pavkovic—'We Can for Sure Execute' Pullout Plan," June 10, 1999, *FBIS* translated text, FTS19990610000549.

But within a month Milosevic's position changed. He no longer wanted an escalation of the conflict. He asked to stop the war.[3]

INVASION APPEARED A MORE DISTANT THREAT

Whatever their appetite for a ground confrontation, Milosevic and his military advisers probably regarded invasion as a more distant threat—one that would provide weeks of strategic warning before it evolved. They were undoubtedly aware from Western press coverage that there was no consensus for a ground campaign within either the United States or NATO. Indeed, as late as June 2, the Western press was reporting that the U.S. Secretary of Defense and the members of the Joint Chiefs of Staff continued to believe that there was "insufficient domestic and international political support for sending ground troops into Kosovo" and therefore remained strongly opposed to such a course of action.[4]

---

[3]See Yeltsin, 2000, p. 264.

[4]See Steven Lee Myers, "U.S. Military Chiefs Firm: No Ground Force for Kosovo," *New York Times*, June 3, 1999, p. A14. Secretary Cohen reports that a majority of the U.S. Congress "was opposed to the land campaign." He considered a land campaign to be "very difficult" because of the terrain:

> There were bridges [that] could have been dropped, with Milosevic's forces up in the hills, just zeroing down on our forces. There could have been substantial casualties. I am convinced it would have turned into quite a contentious issue up on the Hill. At that point, holding the support of Capitol Hill as well as within the coalition would have been quite a challenge.

He also reports there was also no consensus within the Alliance for a ground campaign:

> It was never a close call in getting a consensus to put land forces in. There may have been one or two countries that said they'd be supportive. But out of the 19 total, I doubt very much whether we could have gotten the consensus. I'm convinced we could not have. . . . There were vast differences in cultural, historical, religious, and economic ties to that region. It would have been very difficult to get the support of countries that were under enormous domestic pressure to not even participate in any way in Kosovo. . . . Those who said if we had only led, others would have followed, fail to appreciate the intensity of the opposition within those countries. We were able to hold the consensus for the air campaign under very trying circumstances for many countries. (Interview with Secretary of Defense William Cohen, PBS *Frontline*, "War in Europe," February 22, 2000, http://www.pbs.org/wgbh/pages/frontline/shows/kosovo/interviews.)

The Serb leaders also knew that NATO did not yet have sufficient forces in the theater to conduct such a ground invasion and that it would take two to three months, according to Western estimates, to deploy an adequate force to the area. General Pavkovic, the Third Army commander, claimed that NATO would have required a force of 300,000 to "successfully invade."[5] This estimate was substantially larger than the 150,000 to 175,000 troops that NATO commanders actually thought would be necessary to expel the Serb forces from Kosovo.[6]

However, NATO commanders would have agreed with General Pavkovic's assertion that the forces that NATO had available in Albania and Macedonia in June 1999 were inadequate for a successful invasion.[7] The armored and artillery forces the United States had deployed to Albania to protect the Apache attack helicopters based there were relatively modest. Aside from its 24 attack helicopters, Task Force Hawk had 14 M-1 tanks, 42 M-2 infantry fighting vehicles, 12 artillery pieces, 27 multiple-launch rocket system (MLRS) launchers, and 6000-plus soldiers.[8] The NATO force deployed in Macedonia had only nine battalions, "with about 40 odd tanks and about as many serious artillery pieces—in hardware terms about a tenth of the size" of the Serb forces in Kosovo. According to General

---

[5]This estimate was based on Pavkovic's inflated claim that the Serbs would have had a force of 150,000 men to defend against an invasion. When asked in an interview for his reaction to the possibility of an invasion, Pavkovic said:

> As things were at that time, it was not possible for them to invade. We had 150,000 men, and it would have taken them at least twice that much to successfully invade. If it ever came to face-to-face ground war, it would have been us as the winners. We were prepared to die for Kosovo. There would have been terrible casualties, and we knew that NATO was not prepared to even risk that. They basically supported ground activities of the terrorists.

See Interview with General Pavkovic, February 22, 2000.

[6]See U.K. Ministry of Defence, June 2000, Chapter 8, p. 2.

[7]General Pavkovic stated: "The forces that NATO had available in Albania and Macedonia at the time would never have defeated us." See Antic, August 26, 1999.

[8]See Lust, July 1999, "Task Force Hawk Overview."

Jackson, its commander, the Macedonian-based force "was in no way a competent force to fight an opposed entry."[9]

INDICATIONS THAT GROUND ATTACK WAS BEING CONTEMPLATED PROBABLY WORRIED BELGRADE LEADERS

Even if an invasion was not imminent, the possibility of a future ground attack probably played a role in Milosevic's calculations.[10] He had been told by the Russians that an invasion was coming, and there was increasing speculation about a ground option in Washington and some other NATO capitals. On May 18, President

---

[9]Lieutenant General Sir Mike Jackson, "KFOR: The Inside Story," *RUSI Journal*, February 2000, p. 15.

[10]The conclusion that the threat of invasion probably played a role in Milosevic's decision is largely a matter of inference. The author is aware of little evidence from credible Serb sources that the prospect of a future NATO ground attack was a significant factor in Milosevic's decision to accept NATO's terms on June 3. Milosevic does not mention invasion as being a factor in his decision, and the Serb military and civilian officials cited in this study who were conversant with Milosevic's thinking and who were interviewed shortly after the June 3 decision make no mention of it either. Officials from the General Accounting Office (GAO), however, interviewed one "senior Yugoslav civilian official in Kosovo" (identity otherwise undisclosed) who stated that the fear of a NATO ground invasion was a "primary factor" in the Belgrade leadership's decision to withdraw from Kosovo.

> According to the senior Yugoslav official, the fear of a NATO ground invasion, combined with the timely offer from Russia's envoy, was the primary factor in the withdrawal of Yugoslav forces from the province. According to this official, the Yugoslav leadership believed that NATO would invade Kosovo if the air campaign alone could not defeat Yugoslav forces and feared that an invasion would result in Yugoslavia losing Kosovo completely. This official said that the Yugoslav leadership saw the offer of Russia's envoy as the best possible option, deciding that it was better to withdraw than be conquered, if NATO honored the proposed agreement.

The GAO personnel apparently interviewed this official at an office in Pristina, Kosovo, during one of their two visits to Europe in July 1999, or in October and November 1999. See U.S. GAO, *Balkans Security: Current and Projected Factors Affecting Regional Stability*, Briefing Report, GAO/NSIAD-00-125BR, July 24, 2000.

Both Doder and Branson and Daalder and O'Hanlon, in their accounts of the Kosovo conflict, conclude that the threat of an invasion was a key factor in Milosevic's decision to accede to NATO's peace terms. However, these authors cite no Serb sources to support this assertion. (See Doder and Branson, 1999, p. 271, and Daalder and O'Hanlon, 2000, pp. 203–204.)

Clinton altered his previous commitment not to put U.S. troops into Kosovo by stating that no options should be taken off the table.[11] Task Force Hawk contained elements of a corps headquarters around which substantial ground reinforcements could be deployed, and NATO had announced its intention to increase its peacekeeping forces (KFOR, Kosovo Force) in the area to between 45,000 and 50,000 troops.[12] There was also evidence that NATO forces in Albania had begun to repair the bridges and roads that would be needed to support an invasion force.[13] These indicators strengthened the perception that the NATO allies might be preparing to eventually invade Yugoslavia if that is what it took to win.

Despite the bold rhetoric of military leaders such as General Pavkovic about prevailing over a NATO ground force by extracting unacceptable casualties, Milosevic and his colleagues would have found the prospect of an invasion extremely threatening. They recognized that any NATO ground attack might not be limited to Kosovo but could move on Belgrade, and thereby bring down their regime and directly endanger their personal safety and freedom.

SERB LEADERS MAY HAVE REALIZED THAT INVASION WOULD BE PRECEDED BY INTENSIFIED BOMBING

As of June 2, however, Milosevic appears to have been clearly more concerned about the threat to his power from an intensified NATO bombing campaign than about the possible consequences of a still-distant invasion. Indeed, it is possible that the increasing talk of a possible future NATO ground invasion may have added credence to

---

[11]In his speech to the nation announcing the start of the bombing on March 24, the president had said: "I do not intend to put our troops in Kosovo to fight a war." See R. W. Apple, Jr., "A Domestic Sort with Global Worries," *New York Times*, August 25, 1999, p. A1.

[12]According to the UK's Air Marshal Day, the decision to increase KFOR was, aside from being "militarily right in itself," a "form of heavy breathing on Milosevic" and a subtle way of preparing for an invasion while keeping the coalition together. See Peter Beaumont and Patrick Westover, "Leaks in NATO—and Plan Bravo Minus," *London Sunday Observer*, July 18, 1999.

[13]On May 28, a NATO spokesman announced work on the Albanian road network, noting the "dual-use" potential for carrying NATO ground troops. See PBS *Frontline*, "War in Europe," a Kosovo chronology, February 22, 2000, http://www.pbs.org/wgbh/pages/frontline/shows/kosovo/etc./cron.html.

concerns about a greatly intensified bombing campaign. It may have encouraged Serb leaders to conclude (1) that NATO was bound and determined to win no matter what the cost, (2) that the NATO allies, because of their reluctance to commit ground troops, would broaden and intensify their coercive bombing in hopes of obviating the need for an invasion, and (3) that a devastating aerial preparation of the battlefield in both Kosovo and Serbia proper would undoubtedly precede any NATO ground attack.

Chapter Ten

HE BELIEVED NATO'S TERMS PROVIDED HIM WITH SOME POLITICAL COVER

The terms embodied in Security Council Resolution 1244 of June 10, 1999, and the military-technical agreement between the international security force (KFOR) and the FRY and Serbian governments that preceded it met both NATO's basic demands and Milosevic's need to demonstrate that the FRY had gained at least some concessions in return for its absorption of 11 weeks of bombing.[1] The key operative portions of Security Council Resolution 1244 were contained in Annex 2, the agreement formally accepted by Milosevic on June 3, 1999.[2]

The Security Council resolution and military-technical agreement satisfied the five conditions for a cessation of the bombing laid down by NATO on April 6: (1) a verifiable cessation of combat activities and killings; (2) the withdrawal of FRY and Serb military, police, and paramilitary forces from Kosovo; (3) an agreement to the deployment of an international security force; (4) the unconditional return of all refugees and unimpeded access for humanitarian aid; and (5) agreement to join in putting in place a political framework for Kosovo on the basis of the Rambouillet accords. Although specified

---

[1]The military-technical agreement was signed on June 9, 1999. See United Nations Security Council, letter dated June 15, 1999, from the Secretary-General addressed to the president of the Security Council. Enclosure: military-technical agreement between the international security force (KFOR) and the governments of the Federal Republic of Yugoslavia and the Republic of Serbia, June 9, 1999.

[2]See United Nations Resolution 1244 (1999), adopted by the Security Council at its 4011th meeting on June 10, 1999.

in the Security Council resolution, the fifth condition remains unrealized, as it requires the active cooperation of the Belgrade government.

Most important, NATO clearly prevailed on the security issues Milosevic had fought most bitterly: The Security Council mandated that "all" FRY and Serb forces be withdrawn and that an international security presence with "substantial" NATO participation "be deployed under unified command and control."

RAMBOUILLET COMPARED TO THE JUNE 10 AGREEMENT

In terms of the withdrawal of FRY and Serbian forces, the June agreements were more stringent than Rambouillet. Whereas the Rambouillet text specified a drawdown of VJ and MUP forces over a period of 180 to 365 days, the new military-technical agreement required a complete withdrawal of all forces within 11 days. So, too, the number of FRY and Serb government personnel that will eventually be permitted to return to Kosovo under the Security Council resolution was set at "hundreds not thousands," a smaller number than the 2500 border guards, 75 police, and 50 customs agents envisaged in the Rambouillet accord.[3]

Resolution 1244 also did not specify the areas of "competence" that the FRY and the Republic of Serbia would continue to enjoy in Kosovo as had the Rambouillet terms. Among other areas, Rambouillet had accorded the FRY "competence" over maintaining a common market within the FRY, monetary policy, defense, foreign policy, customs services, federal taxation, and federal elections.[4]

From the all-important standpoint of FRY sovereignty, however, Milosevic had reason to argue that the terms embodied in Security Council Resolution 1244 were an improvement over the terms contained in the Rambouillet Agreement.

---

[3]Under Resolution 1244, the FRY and Serbian personnel will be permitted to return to Kosovo to perform the following functions: "Liaison with the international civil mission and the international security presence; marking/clearing minefields; maintaining a presence at Serb patrimonial sites; and maintaining a presence at key border crossings."

[4]See Rambouillet Agreement, Chapter 1, "Constitution," Article I (3).

First, the sweeping and humiliating rights of "transit, bivouac, maneuver, billet, utilization," and infrastructure modification throughout the FRY accorded to NATO forces by the Rambouillet text were now absent. The June military-technical agreement granted NATO forces passage and access only to Kosovo proper.

Second, Resolution 1244 omitted any suggestion that the final status of Kosovo might be determined even in part by a referendum or by some other ascertainment "of the will of the people," as had been implied by the article added to the Rambouillet text at the KLA's insistence. While the resolution specified that the "political process towards the establishment of an interim framework agreement providing for substantial self-government for Kosovo" should take "full account of the Rambouillet accords," it coupled this admonishment with the requirement that the political process also take full account of "the principles of sovereignty and territorial integrity of the Federal Republic of Yugoslavia. . . . "[5] While the "sovereignty and territorial integrity" of the FRY was reaffirmed in the preamble and Chapter 7, Article I, (1a) of the Rambouillet text, it was not explicitly mentioned as a basis for determining "a mechanism for a final settlement for Kosovo."[6] The Security Council formulation would seem to rule out Rambouillet providing a path to Kosovo independence.

Third, the Security Council resolution specified that the United Nations would control the implementation of the international civil presence in Kosovo, whereas the Rambouillet accords had assigned this function to the OSCE, in cooperation with the EU. Milosevic had pressed hard to make the United Nations the controlling body of the security and civil presence in Kosovo both because he believed the conflict in Bosnia-Herzegovina had shown U.N. officials to be vulnerable to Serb manipulation and because he thought Russia would be better positioned to protect the FRY's interests in a body where it

---

[5]Article 8, Annex 2, Resolution 1244 calls for "a political process towards the establishment of an interim political agreement providing for substantial self-government for Kosovo, taking full account of the Rambouillet accords and the principles of sovereignty and territorial integrity of the Federal Republic of Yugoslavia and the other countries of the region, and the demilitarization of UCK. Negotiations between the parties for a settlement should not delay or disrupt the establishment of democratic self-governing institutions."

[6]See Rambouillet Agreement, Chapter 8, Article I, (3).

enjoyed the veto. While NATO refused to agree to FRY and Russian demands that the U.N. have operational control of the security presence, it did agree to U.N. control of the civil presence.[7]

MILOSEVIC PROCLAIMED VICTORY

Milosevic alluded to these improved terms in his June 10 television address to the nation that followed the cessation of hostilities. Proclaiming that the "aggression" was over and that "peace" had prevailed over "violence," Milosevic went on to claim that the future of Kosovo had now been secured:

> Early this year, numerous rallies were held throughout the country. Their united message was we shall not give up Kosovo. We have not given up Kosovo. The Group of Eight most developed countries of the world and the United Nations guarantee the sovereignty and territorial integrity of our country. This guarantee is also contained in the draft resolution. The Belgrade agreement has closed the open issues of the possible independence of Kosovo at the time prior to the aggression. The territorial entirety of our country cannot be threatened. We have persevered and succeeded in defending the country because we brought the entire problem to the summit of the world authority—the United Nations—and handed its resolution to be sought under UN auspices and in keeping with the UN Charter. The international forces being deployed in Kosovo with the task of equally ensuring the safety of all citizens will be under UN auspices, as will be the political process, which will be based on the principles which stem from previously conducted discussions, but are also equally based on the sovereignty and territorial integrity of our country. This means that only autonomy, and nothing else outside that, can be mentioned in this political process.[8]

---

[7] Under the Rambouillet Agreement, the Security Council was to be "invited to pass a resolution under Chapter VII of the Charter endorsing and adopting the arrangements set forth" in Chapter 7, Implementation II. Otherwise, Rambouillet was mute on the subject of the United Nations. See Chapter 7, Article I, (1a).

[8] Milosevic also celebrated his success in promoting a U.N. role in the settlement as a boon to the "entire-freedom-loving world." By insisting on the U.N. role, "we were not only defending our country but have brought the UN back to the world stage." He claimed this "is our contribution to the world: to prevent the creation of a unipolar world, to prevent the acceptance of a world based on the diktat from one center." See "Yugoslav President Slobodan Milosevic's Address to the Nation," Belgrade *Borba*, June 10, 1999.

Other Belgrade officials echoed these themes in their statements. But the government's spin masters could not mask the facts that the FRY could no longer protect the Serbs in Kosovo, the majority of whom were already beginning to flee to Serbia; that NATO commanded and controlled the armed presence in Kosovo and provided the bulk of its forces; and that the Kosovo Albanians, including elements of the KLA, were likely to govern Kosovo in the manner of an independent, sovereign state. There can be little question that the agreements Milosevic was forced to accept in June 1999 left the FRY, the Serb Republic, and the Kosovo Serbs with far less presence and power in Kosovo than the type of agreement that Milosevic could almost certainly have secured prior to 1999 had he possessed the wit to seek and observe such an accord.

Part III

CONCLUDING OBSERVATIONS

Chapter Eleven

CONCLUDING OBSERVATIONS

AIR POWER'S CONTRIBUTIONS WERE CRUCIAL

As the preceding discussion has shown, several interrelated factors shaped Milosevic's decision to accept NATO's terms for war termination on June 3. Among the most important was the Belgrade regime's failure to gain leverage on NATO through its prosecution of ethnic cleansing, exploitation of Serbian civilian casualties, attempts to impose losses on NATO aircraft and aircrews, and play of the "Russian card." Ethnic cleansing proved counterproductive to the Serb cause in that it strengthened rather than weakened NATO's unity and resolve; the anticipated NATO air losses never materialized; and Russia's diplomatic support of the FRY eventually dissolved, leaving Belgrade totally isolated.

However, it was the cumulative impact of NATO air power and the future threat it posed that most influenced Milosevic's eventual decision to come to terms. Air power made three crucial contributions to the conflict's successful outcome.

First, the NATO bombing created a political climate in Serbia conducive to concessions on Kosovo. By the end of the air campaign, the Serbian citizens and politicians who had initially overwhelmingly opposed giving in to NATO's demands had increasingly come to the view that Milosevic had to make whatever concessions were necessary to get the air attacks stopped. Concessions that would have been politically dangerous for Milosevic to have accepted in March could be justified by the beginning of June—even to the Serbian military and the extreme nationalists—as a necessary price for halting the bombing.

Second, the bombing, as it intensified, eventually stimulated a growing interest on the part of Milosevic and his associates to end the conflict. They perceived the air attacks as (1) causing a magnitude of damage to Serbia's infrastructure, economy, and political stability that, if allowed to continue, might eventually threaten their regime's survival, and (2) creating stress, hardships, and costs for members of their own ruling elite. The greatest pressures for war termination were caused by NATO's attacks on "dual-use" fixed targets in Serbia.

Third, the perception that NATO's future air attacks would be unconstrained made a settlement seem imperative. When presented with what they perceived to be a NATO ultimatum endorsed by Russia on June 2, Milosevic and his colleagues concluded that NATO, if its terms were rejected, was poised to launch a "fierce" and unconstrained bombing campaign that would destroy Serbia's entire remaining infrastructure, including the many as yet unstruck infrastructure targets in Belgrade. Not only would this leave much of the country's economy in ruins, but it would also create enormous hardships for the Serb public. Milosevic apparently calculated that the public would neither long tolerate nor forgive him for the hardships that would result from such an intensified bombing campaign, particularly if its more extreme effects—such as a continuous, nationwide power outage—carried over into the harsh Balkan winter. He therefore concluded that a continued refusal to make peace would likely cost him his hold on power.

Air attacks also provided the spur to prevent Serb stalling and backsliding during the military-technical negotiations that preceded the June 10 cease-fire. When the military-technical talks bogged down, the intensity of NATO air strikes picked up.[1]

---

[1]Aside from demanding that they be granted more time to remove their forces from Kosovo—a request to which the NATO authorities partly acceded by increasing the withdrawal deadline from seven to eleven days—the Serb negotiators at the technical talks also attempted to "water down" some of the terms Milosevic had accepted on June 3 regarding the number of Serb policemen to be allowed in Kosovo, the buffer area in Serbia beyond which Serbian forces would be withdrawn, and whether returning refugees would be required to go through Serbian immigration and customs con-

Finally, air power provided crucial humanitarian support when it was badly needed. The U.S. airlift to the region, which provided food, tents, and sleeping gear to the refugees during the early days of the mass exodus from Kosovo, helped ease the humanitarian crises in Albania and Macedonia until other aid could arrive.

While there has been much criticism of the constraints governing the approval of targets and the ROEs imposed during the air campaign, it is important to recognize that NATO's air operations were conducted in a manner that successfully confounded Milosevic's attempts to erode support for the war in the allied countries. The measures NATO leaders adopted to avoid allied KIAs and POWs and to hold down enemy civilian casualties and collateral damage were crucial to limiting active opposition to the war in countries such as Italy, Greece, and Germany, where important political constituencies harbored significant doubts about the NATO bombing.[2] Civilian casualties were a particularly sensitive issue for Chancellor Gerhard Schroeder's coalition government in Germany, which depended on continued support from its coalition partner, the formerly pacifist Green Party, to remain in office. This political reality made the Bonn government particularly eager for a resolution of the conflict.[3]

Maintaining Alliance cohesion was a major objective of the NATO commanders and was a sine qua non of their eventual success.[4]

---

trol See Elizabeth Becker, "Kosovo Talks Break Down As Serbs Balk over Details; NATO Will Step Up Bombing"; Craig R. Whitney, "Allies Say Bombing Will Intensify After Serbs Balk at Signing Pullout Proposal," *New York Times*, June 7, 1999, pp. A1, A10, and A11; Carlotta Gall, "Serbs Raise an Obstacle to Return of Refugees," *New York Times*, June 9, 1999, p. A13; and David R. Sands, "Yugoslavia Capitulates; Air War May Stop Today, Accord Meets NATO's Demands," *Washington Times*, June 10, 1999, pp. A1 and A12.

[2]For a discussion of how the Alliance partners tended to view the Kosovo war from often "sharply different perspectives," see Alan Cowell, "It's a Wonder This Alliance Is Unified," *New York Times*, April 25, 1999, p. Wk 5.

[3]On May 13, 1999, the Greens, in a bitterly divisive and stormy congress, rejected a motion for "an immediate and unconditional termination of the NATO bombing," which probably would have brought down the Schroeder government. Instead, the Greens adopted a substitute motion calling for a "limited halt" to the bombing, which was adopted by 444 votes to 318. See Roger Cohen, "In a Breach, German Party Backs 'Limited Halt' in Kosovo Air War," *New York Times*, May 14, 1999, pp. A1 and A13.

[4]According to General Wesley Clark, NATO supreme allied commander, there were four "measures of merit" that shaped the selection of targets: "One was to avoid the loss of NATO aircraft. The second was to impact Serb forces on the ground. The third

Even though temporary bombing halts had been proposed by several allied governments, NATO was steadfast in keeping the pressure on Milosevic. Indeed, it was the eventual escalation of the bombing in May that brought about the increased propensity of Milosevic and his associates to yield and made the prospect of unconstrained future bombing credible had they refused NATO's settlement terms.

THE CONDITIONS PROMPTING THE SERBS TO SETTLE WERE ALSO EVIDENT IN OTHER CONFLICTS

Commentators have suggested that Operation Allied Force lies outside the mainstream of the U.S. experience with the coercive use of air power in that it was conducted in the absence of a simultaneous ground battle. Some commentators even contend that this was the "first time" air attacks have played a crucial role in persuading enemy decisionmakers to come to terms. Contrary to such assertions, the evidence suggests that the military pressures and other conditions that forced Milosevic to come to terms generally paralleled the military pressures and conditions that compelled enemy leaders in other past conflicts to capitulate or agree to negotiated settlements acceptable to the United States.

Analyses of past conflicts have shown that air attacks or threatened air attacks have helped persuade enemy decisionmakers to terminate conflicts on terms acceptable to the United States when the enemy leaders perceived that:

- their military forces no longer possessed a viable, near-term offensive option and faced stalemate or eventual defeat on the battlefield

- they were unlikely to get better peace terms if they prolonged the fighting

- they had no prospect of mounting an effective defense against the air attacks or of compelling a stop to the coercive bombing

---

was to minimize collateral damage and the fourth was to maintain Alliance cohesion." See "Clark Looks Back on Kosovo Conflict," *Defense Week*, August 23, 1999, p. 7.

- the cost of the damage from future attacks was likely to significantly outweigh the costs of the concessions the United States was demanding.[5]

All these conditions prevailed at the time U.S. air attacks or the threat of air attacks helped force war termination with Japan in 1945, Korea in 1953, Vietnam in 1973, Iraq in 1991, and the Bosnian Serbs in 1995.[6] In each instance, it was more the damage that the enemy decisionmakers feared would be inflicted in the future than the damage they had already absorbed that drove the U.S. enemies to a settlement.

These conditions also prevailed in the case of Serbia in 1999. While FRY ground forces had not yet been defeated on the battlefield, they were clearly stalemated in that they had no viable options for bringing military pressure to bear on the NATO countries attacking them. Milosevic had no reason to believe that his bargaining position would improve with time and had, in fact, been told that NATO's subsequent offers would be less generous than the June 2 proposal. Milosevic recognized that the VJ had no defense against NATO's aircraft and missile strikes on fixed targets and could impose little if any cost on their attackers. Finally, Milosevic apparently calculated that the loss of Kosovo would be less dangerous to his ultimate survival in power than would be the consequences of an unconstrained bombing attack that razed Serbia to the ground.

MILOSEVIC'S DECISION TO YIELD DEPENDED ON DEVELOPMENTS THAT TOOK TIME TO MATURE

It has been suggested that a more robust bombing of infrastructure and other fixed targets in Belgrade at the outset of the conflict would have significantly reduced the time it took to bring Milosevic to terms.

---

[5]For the author's analysis of the role air attacks have played in shaping enemy war termination decisions since World War II, see Stephen T. Hosmer, *Psychological Effects of U.S. Air Operations in Four Wars 1941–1991: Lessons for U.S. Commanders*, Santa Monica: RAND, MR-576-AF, 1996, p. 74.

[6]Op. cit., pp. 9–67.

Lieutenant General Michael Short, the air component commander, believes that NATO should "have gone for the head of the snake on the first night." Had he had the freedom of action to do so, he would have "turned the lights out" in Belgrade, dropped the city's bridges across the Danube, and "hit five or six political-military headquarters in downtown Belgrade." Striking Milosevic "hard the first night and [staying] after him, regardless of the weather" would have caused Milosevic to reassess the likely costs of his Kosovo policy. "The questioning would have started right away: 'If this is what the first night is like, what's the rest of it going to be like?'"[7]

General Short believes that an intense and sustained attack would have forced Milosevic to come to terms within three to four weeks.[8] Certainly, valid arguments can be made that going "downtown" from the outset could have significantly shortened the war. Among other effects, the type of campaign General Short advocates would have imposed immediate hardships on Milosevic's associates and other members of the Belgrade public and would have demonstrated NATO's resolve to prevail, even if this required major damage to Serbia's infrastructure.

However, it is by no means certain that even if it had been politically feasible, going downtown at the outset would have shortened the conflict to the extent expected by General Short. Milosevic's decision to yield depended in part on developments that took time to mature. It is unclear, for example, that an immediate attack on Belgrade's electric power and bridges would have greatly accelerated Russia's eventual decision to abandon its objections to NATO's settlement terms. Nor is it clear that such attacks would have disabused

---

[7]As a result of his earlier face-to-face dealings with Milosevic, General Short had concluded that "if you hit that man hard, slapped him up the side of the head, he'd pay attention." See Senate Committee on Armed Services hearing on "Lessons Learned from Military Operations and Relief Efforts in Kosovo," October 21, 1999, for General Short's testimony therein.

[8]Interview with Lieutenant General Michael Short, Wright-Patterson AFB, Dayton, Ohio, February 2, 2000. General Short's view was shared by other airmen. Senator James M. Inhofe, after making several trips to Ramstein, concluded that an intensified air campaign could have produced success within a quarter or a third of the (11-week) time it actually took. See Senate Committee on Armed Services hearing on "Lessons Learned from Military Operations and Relief Efforts in Kosovo," October 21, 1999, for the statement by Senator Inhofe.

Milosevic of his expectation that the humanitarian crisis caused by ethnic cleansing or the accumulating civilian casualties caused by the bombing would eventually erode NATO's resolve to continue the air campaign. It should also be recalled that an important ingredient of the war weariness that eventually invaded the Serbian public was the cumulative stress caused by daily air raid alerts.

It is also unclear whether going "downtown" immediately might have served to dampen rather than intensify Serb fears of NATO escalation. Attacking Belgrade heavily from the outset might have had the perverse effect of "killing the hostage"—that is, causing enough damage to convince the Serb leaders that they had little to lose by holding out longer.

Proponents of going "downtown" point to the Gulf War as the model for how coercive air operations should be conducted. Baghdad was accorded different treatment from Belgrade in that coalition attacks in 1991 "turned out the lights" in the Iraqi capital on the first night. The telephone exchanges and some of the bridges in Baghdad were also eventually struck, whereas similar targets were never attacked in Belgrade. However, the total number of targets attacked in each capital was comparable and relatively small. Moreover, going downtown on the first night of the Gulf War did not produce early war termination. The conflict continued for some 42 days before ending in a coalition ground campaign.[9]

In any case, whatever its merits might have been, attacking Belgrade in a robust manner at the outset of the war was never a feasible option. General Short is the first to "recognize the political limitations that kept [NATO] from going downtown the first night."[10] Indeed, even though air planners had "verified between 250 and 300 valid, solid military targets," he was postured to strike only about 90 targets

---

[9]The key contribution of the coalition air campaign in Operation Desert Storm was to cause the Iraqi troops in the Kuwait Theater of Operations (KTO) to desert their positions and lose their will to fight, thereby denying the Iraqi forces the ability to inflict significant numbers of U.S. casualties and resist the coalition ground attack. See Hosmer, 1996, pp. 141–175.

[10]See Senate Committee on Armed Services Hearing on "Lessons Learned from Military Operations and Relief Efforts in Kosovo," October 21, 1999, for General Short's testimony therein.

the first three nights.   General Short reports that he "kept getting instructed":

> Mike, you're only going to be allowed to bomb two, maybe three nights. That's all Washington can stand, and that's all some members of the alliance can stand. That's why you've only got 90 targets. This will be over in three nights.[11]

The NATO allies had resorted to bombing only reluctantly and were convinced that only a minimum amount of force would be necessary to persuade Milosevic to come to terms. They wanted to limit the damage to Serbia and agreed to attack sensitive targets such as electric power in Belgrade only when it became apparent that lesser measures would not suffice to bring about a settlement.[12]

NATO AND SERB LEADERS PERCEIVED STRATEGIC BOMBING DIFFERENTLY

There was a striking incongruity between Serb and NATO perceptions of the air campaign. Even though NATO commanders accepted the need to minimize civilian casualties and collateral damage, they nevertheless felt their air operations were overly constrained. They believed the efficiency and potential effectiveness of their air operations were significantly hindered by the slow release or outright denial of lucrative strategic targets, particularly in Belgrade.[13]

As General Short described the situation, "political constraints existed throughout the conflict":

---

[11]See Interview with Lieutenant General Michael Short, PBS *Frontline*, "War in Europe," February 22, 2000, http://www.pbs.org/wgbh/pages/frontline/shows/kosovo/interviews.

[12]For a discussion of the reluctance of some NATO allies to destroy Serbia, see Interview with General Klaus Naumann, Chairman of NATO's Military Committee, PBS *Frontline*, "War in Europe," February 22, 2000, http://www.pbs.org/wgbh/pages/frontline/shows/kosovo/interviews.

[13]Among the targets that were never cleared for attack but that General Short felt were legitimate and important targets were several political-military headquarters and the Danube River bridges in Belgrade as well as a number of dual-use factories and electric power stations. See Interview with Lieutenant General Michael Short, February 22, 2000.

There were targets that individual nations would not let us hit, or wouldn't let us hit with airplanes launched from their soil. There were targets that individual nations would not hit themselves, but it was okay for somebody else to hit. Apparently, and clearly, it was relayed to me that every nation had a vote. An individual nation could say: you can't hit that target.[14]

NATO commanders also chafed under the increasingly tight ROEs that were imposed on allied air operations after bombing errors. In Kosovo, NATO pilots were eventually prohibited from attacking suspected VJ trucks or headquarters buildings for fear of harming civilians. After the Chinese Embassy was accidentally attacked on May 7, no new targets were allowed to be struck within a five-mile radius of Belgrade's center.[15]

As previously discussed, the Serb view of the NATO air campaign was entirely different. The Serbs perceived NATO's attacks to be intentionally directed at civilian as well as military targets. Most important, Milosevic and his colleagues believed that NATO had both the intent and the freedom of action to destroy their country's entire infrastructure if need be. This distorted perception of the allied threat greatly benefited NATO when it came to persuading Milosevic to accept its terms for war termination—for had Serb perceptions of the air campaign more closely paralleled the views of the NATO commanders, the conflict might have continued longer.

---

[14]Ibid. In actual practice, it was the five major NATO powers, or Quint (the United States, the United Kingdom, France, Germany, and Italy), that had the paramount say on targets. See Steven Lee Myers, "All in Favor of This Target, Say Yes, Si, Oui, Ja," *New York Times*, April 25, 1999, p. Wk 4.

[15]After Serbian civilians were killed during an attack on a bridge near Nis, the "guidance for attacking bridges in the future was: You will no longer attack bridges in daylight. You will no longer attack bridges on weekends or market days or holidays. In fact, you'll only attack bridges between 10:00 at night and 4:00 in the morning." See Senate Committee on Armed Services Hearing on "Lessons Learned from Military Operations and Relief Efforts in Kosovo," October 21, 1999, for General Short's testimony therein.

MAINTAINING CAPABILITIES TO COERCE FUTURE ADVERSARY LEADERS

While not necessarily a template for future U.S. military operations, Operation Allied Force was nonetheless conducted under constraints that are likely to be present in future conflicts. In order to maximize the coercive effects of air power in situations similar to that encountered in Kosovo, the United States will need to continue to develop improved capabilities to locate, identify, and rapidly strike (with minimal civilian casualties) mobile targets in terrain that favors the hider. Because attacks on "dual-use" infrastructure targets may be the most effective way to coerce enemy decisionmakers, the United States must not assume binding international obligations that could subject U.S. persons to possible prosecution for attacking targets that responsible U.S. legal authorities have certified to be legitimate military targets.

Improve Capabilities to Attack Dispersed and Hidden Forces

NATO's attempts to "systematically" and "progressively" destroy the FRY's military forces and thereby pressure Milosevic to come to terms proved largely unsuccessful. The Serbs were able to preserve intact the vast bulk of their ground forces by dispersing them before the bombing began and by making extensive use of concealment, camouflage, and hardened underground shelters. They were also able to shield their forces from attack by locating them among civilian facilities and populations. Because Serb forces did not have to concentrate, maneuver in large formations, or sustain a high tempo of operations in order to accomplish their missions, these tactics were successful. It can be assumed that future adversaries will resort to similar measures to limit the destructive effects of friendly air power on their ground forces when the battlefield situation permits such actions.

To counter such tactics, the United States and its allies must seek to develop sensors, surveillance and reconnaissance platforms, target processing and dynamic control measures, weapon systems, and concepts of operation that will improve their capabilities to attack enemy armored and artillery forces when such forces are widely dispersed, hidden under foliage, or located in civilian settings. To minimize civilian casualties and collateral damage, extremely accurate low-yield munitions will be required to attack enemy military forces located in or near civilian structures. Special munitions will also be required to effectively attack enemy leadership and C^3 facilities that are located deep underground.

Whenever feasible, allied air campaigns against enemy ground forces should be accompanied by the credible threat of an allied ground attack. The presence of an allied ground threat will cause enemy forces to concentrate and thereby become richer targets for air attack. In addition, the presence of an allied ground threat will heighten the enemy leaders' concerns that their continued resistance might eventually invite their overthrow and punishment by allied invasion forces.

Preserve Option to Attack "Dual-Use" Infrastructure Targets

In the Kosovo conflict, it was the attacks and threat of attacks on "dual-use" infrastructure targets that generated the decisive pressure for war termination. However, the freedom of action to attack similar targets in future conflicts could become circumscribed because of U.S. and allied leaders' concerns about being prosecuted as "war criminals" or an inability to attack such targets without significant civilian casualties.

During and after the 1999 NATO bombing campaign, the prosecutor of the U.N.-established International Criminal Tribunal for the Former Yugoslavia (ICTY) received "numerous requests" that she investigate and indict the "senior political and military figures from NATO countries" who were alleged to have "committed serious violations of international humanitarian law during the campaign." Criticisms of the NATO bombing included allegations that "NATO forces deliberately attacked civilian infrastructure targets (and that such attacks were unlawful), deliberately or recklessly attacked the civilian population, and deliberately or recklessly caused excessive civilian casualties in disregard of the rule of proportionality by trying to fight a 'zero casualty' war for their own side."[16] The ICTY committee asked to look into these allegations found insufficient grounds for an in-depth investigation of these charges, holding either that the law was "not sufficiently clear" or that further investigations were unlikely to produce "sufficient evidence to substantiate the charges."[17]

However, two prominent NGOs that assessed the bombing came to less benign conclusions. Human Rights Watch, which conducted an on-the-spot investigation of the civilian damage from the air campaign, found that more than one-half of the estimated 500 civilian deaths caused by the air campaign resulted from attacks on illegitimate or questionable targets, including targets that were "nonmilitary in function."[18] Amnesty International, in its report on the air campaign, went even further, charging that NATO had committed serious violations of the rules of war, unlawful killings, and, in the case of the bombing of Serb Radio and Television in Belgrade, a "war crime."[19]

The fact that such allegations arose in a conflict against a "pariah" regime engaged in massive human rights abuses points to the close

---

[16]See Final Report to the Prosecutor by the Committee Established to Review the NATO Bombing Campaign Against the Federal Republic of Yugoslavia, *I. Background and Mandate*, June 13, 2000, http://www.un.org/icty/pressreal/nato061300.htm.

[17]In the words of the ICTY committee, "NATO has admitted that mistakes did occur during the bombing campaign; errors of judgment may also have occurred. Selection of certain objectives for attack may be subject to legal debate. On the basis of the information reviewed, however, the committee is of the opinion that neither an in-depth investigation related to the bombing campaign as a whole nor investigations related to specific incidents are justified. In all cases, either the law is not sufficiently clear or investigations are unlikely to result in the acquisition of sufficient evidence to substantiate charges against high level accused or against lower accused for particularly heinous offences." See Final Report to the Prosecutor, *V. Recommendations*.

[18]Human Rights Watch concluded that nine of the targets struck were nonmilitary in function; these were the "Serb Radio and Television in Belgrade, the New Belgrade heating plant, and seven bridges that were neither major transportation routes nor had other military functions." See Human Rights Watch, "New Figures on Civilian Deaths in Kosovo War," February 7, 2000, http://www.hrw.org/press/2000/02/nato207.htm, and "Summary, Civilian Deaths in the NATO Air Campaign," February 7, 2000, http://www.hrw.org/reports/2000/nato/Natbm200.htm.

[19]See Robert Fisk, "NATO 'Deliberately Attacked Civilians in Serbia,'" *The Independent Digital* (UK), June 7, 2000, http://www.independent.co.uk/story.jsp?story=18255, and Amnesty International, *NATO/Federal Republic of Yugoslavia, "Collateral Damage" or Unlawful Killings?* June 6, 2000.

and critical scrutiny that is likely to be given to future attacks on "dual-use" infrastructure targets, including attacks on targets similar to those that helped pressure Milosevic to come to terms.[20] Air operations that result in civilian deaths will be subjected to particularly close scrutiny, in part because the increasing availability and capability of precision weapons will foster expectations for minimal collateral damage. Attacks on targets that critics consider to be only marginally related to enemy military operations and that result in civilian casualties will be particularly vulnerable to condemnation and possibly even to legal sanction. The prospect of such condemnation and the possibility that an overzealous or politically motivated international prosecutor might indict them for war crimes may make allied civilian and military leaders reluctant to pursue warfighting strategies that aim in part to coerce enemy leaders through attacks on "dual-use" infrastructure targets.

Attacks on "dual-use" military targets may pose particular risk of legal sanction in that the military utility and therefore the legitimacy of a particular target can differ according to the eye of the beholder. As previously noted, there were differences of view about the legitimacy of particular targets even within the NATO coalition. Reflecting on the legal dilemmas of waging coalition warfare, General Short said:

> There are nations that will not attack targets that my nation will attack. There are nations that do not share with us a definition of what is a valid military target.[21]

It is important to note that all the "dual-use" targets that the legal analysts at Human Rights Watch and Amnesty International criti-

---

[20]Referring to the war crimes allegations, former Secretary of Defense William Cohen stated:

> The very notion that there would be allegations of war crimes, given what we went through to protect innocent life, is I think a shape of some things to come in the way of allegations to come by third parties or nations that would seek to embarrass or hinder our participation in international affairs.

Pamela Hess, "Pentagon Takes Strong Exception to UN Criminal Court," *United Press International*, June 12, 2000.

[21]Remarks by Lieutenant General Michael Short at the Air Force Association's Air Warfare Symposium, February 25, 2000, cited in Amnesty International, June 6, 2000.

cized as being illegitimate and "nonmilitary" in function were deemed legitimate military targets by the legal officials at the NATO and U.S. command echelons that approved the targets to be attacked in Operation Allied Force.

One of the fundamental concerns voiced about the Rome Treaty creating the International Criminal Court (ICC) is that it would expose U.S. civilian and military leaders and other personnel who were acting within the authority of the U.S. government to unwarranted prosecution.[22] Even though the United States signed the Rome Treaty in December 2000, U.S. State Department spokesman Richard Boucher stated that Clinton administration officials shared many of the concerns about the treaty expressed by people in the Congress and did not wish the treaty "to turn into some device that could be used against U.S. leaders or U.S. soldiers or U.S. military people who are acting within the authority of the U.S. government."[23] Secretary of Defense William Cohen was particularly concerned that U.S. soldiers would be subject to "frivolous allegations" and that opportunities to manipulate the court to hamstring the United States would abound.[24] Some critics of the Rome statute argue that if the treaty ever enters force, "American soldiers and officials will be subject to trial and punishment by an international independent prosecutor, backed by judges from countries with legal traditions fundamentally different from our own, and that may actually be hostile to the United States."[25]

---

[22]The principal reservation voiced by U.S. officials about the Rome Treaty is that it would expose U.S. armed forces to prosecution before the ICC even before the United States becomes a party to the treaty. When the United States signed the treaty on December 31, 2000, it purportedly did so in part, according to President Clinton, to maintain its ability to "influence the evolution of the Court." The United States did not abandon its "concerns about significant flaws in the Treaty," and President Clinton recommended that it not be submitted for ratification until fundamental U.S. concerns were satisfied. See Text of President Clinton's December 31 statement authorizing the United States to sign the Treaty on the International Criminal Court, *New York Times*, January 1, 2001, p. A6.

[23]See Richard Boucher, U.S. Department of State Press Briefing, January 2, 2001.

[24]Hess, June 12, 2000.

[25]See Lee Casey and David Rivkin, "Clinton's Worst Folly," *Washington Times*, January 9, 2001, p. A16. One worry voiced by critics is that the Rome statute "provides for no external mechanism of restraint—no constitutional framework of 'checks and balances'—to limit the powers of the court and its prosecutor. Indeed, Article 119 of the Rome statute directs that 'any dispute concerning the judicial functions of the

The fear of being accused of war crimes for honest mistakes that resulted in unintended destruction or for attacking targets that foreign legal authorities deemed to be "nonmilitary" in nature could have a chilling effect on U.S. military actions. Indeed, David J. Scheffer, former U.S. Ambassador at Large for War Crime Issues, warned that a possible

> . . . consequence imposed by Article 12, particularly for nonparties to the Treaty, will be to limit severely those lawful, but highly controversial and inherently risky, interventions that the advocates of human rights and world peace so desperately seek from the United States and other military powers. There will be significant new legal and political risks in such interventions, which up to this point have been mostly shielded from politically motivated charges.[26]

Attacks or threats of attacks on "dual-use" military targets may be the most effective—and in some instances the only feasible way—to coerce enemy decisionmakers to terminate conflicts and crises rapidly on terms acceptable to the United States. Speedy war termination may ultimately save enemy as well as friendly lives. It is therefore important that the United States not assume binding international obligations that could subject U.S. civilian and military persons to

---

court shall be settled by the decision of the court. In the end, the court is its own referee, producing the United States unease as to the directions that a fully empowered permanent court could eventually take." See Michael N. Schmitt and Major Peter J. Richards, U.S. Air Force, "Into Uncharted Waters: The International Criminal Court," *Naval War College Review*, Winter 2000, p. 123. Secretary Cohen made much the same argument, stating:

> Our concern is once you have a totally independent international court that is not under the jurisdiction, supervision or is in any way influenced, obligated or accountable to a supervisory institution like the U.N. Security Council, then the potential for allegations to be made against our soldiers could be frivolous in nature. You could have charges brought before The Hague and this, I think, would be very destructive to our international participation. It would be intolerable as far as our people are concerned. (Hess, June 12, 2000.)

[26]David J. Scheffer, "Deterrence of War Crimes in the 21st Century," address to the Twelfth Annual U.S. Pacific Command International Military Operations and Law Conference, Honolulu, Hawaii, February 23, 1999. See also Scheffer, "Evolution of U.S. Policy Toward the International Criminal Court," address at American University, Washington, D.C., September 14, 2000.

prosecution for attacking targets that responsible U.S. legal authorities have certified to be legitimate military targets. Otherwise, U.S. civilian officials and war fighters may be deterred from conducting effective air campaigns because of the concern that they might be indicted and even convicted as war criminals by prosecutors and jurists who hold to a different view about the legitimacy of certain targets and who may harbor animus toward the United States. Nor should U.S. persons be allowed to be deterred from conducting their military duties by the fear that they will be prosecuted for unintended bombing errors. As Secretary Scheffer put it:

> In any military action, we have to accept the possibility that things will not go as planned—missiles or bombs may go off targets, and human error could result in unintended destruction. But fear of being accused of war crimes for honest mistakes should not prevent us from acting.[27]

But to retain the option to strike "dual-use" targets, it will also be necessary that such attacks be conducted with minimal loss of civilian life and other unintended damage. Military leaders must ensure that U.S. and allied forces possess the precision strike capabilities, training, target intelligence, situational awareness, ROEs, and concepts of operation that will enable those forces to attack "dual-use" as well as other targets with minimal civilian casualties and collateral damage. These capabilities will be needed not only to comply with the laws of war but also to maintain the political support that will be required to sustain U.S. and allied military interventions, particularly when less than vital national interests are at stake. In Operation Allied Force, the ROEs and other actions the allies adopted to hold down civilian casualties were a key factor in sustaining NATO's freedom of action to prosecute the conflict over Kosovo to its successful conclusion.

---

[27]Scheffer, September 14, 2000.

BIBLIOGRAPHY

Address by Ratko Markovic, Serbian Deputy Prime Minister and head of the Serbian delegation at the Rambouillet and Paris negotiations on Kosovo, in the Serbian parliament on March 23, 1999, as reported on Belgrade Radio, March 23, 1999, *FBIS* translated text, FTS19990323001225.

AFP (North European Service), "Gen Pavkovic— 'We Can for Sure Execute' Pullout Plan," June 10, 1999, *FBIS* translated text, FTS19990610000549.

Ahtisaari, Martti, Bonn news conference of June 3, 1999, *New York Times*, June 4, 1999.

Albright, Madeleine K., press conference following meetings on Kosovo, Rambouillet, France, February 23, 1999, as released by the Office of the Spokesman, Paris, France, U.S. Department of State, http://www. secretary.state.gov/statement/1999/990223.html.

Amnesty International, *NATO/Federal Republic of Yugoslavia, "Collateral Damage" or Unlawful Killings?* June 6, 2000.

Anastasijevic, Dejan, "Apres Slobo, the Deluge," *Institute for War and Peace Reporting*, March 24, 1999, http://iwpr.vs4.cerbernet.co.uk/index.pl?archive/bcr/bcr_19990324_1_eng.txt.

Andrew, Christopher, "The Mitrokhin Archive," *RUSI Journal*, February 2000.

Annex I, "Kosovo Case Study," Interagency Review of U.S. Government Civilian Humanitarian and Transition Programs, U.S. Department of State, January 2000.

Antic, Milos, interview with General Nebojsa Pavkovic on Mount Tara, *Nedeljni Telegraf,* August 25, 1999, translated in *FBIS,* East Europe, Balkan States (Serbia, Kosovo), "Gen. Pavkovic Interviewed; Sees Army Return," August 26, 1999. FTS19990826000853.

Antonenko, Oksana, "Russia, NATO and European Security After Kosovo," *Survival,* Winter 1999.

Apple, R. W., Jr., "A Domestic Sort with Global Worries," *New York Times,* August 25, 1999.

Arkin, William M., "Smart Bombs, Dumb Targeting?" *Bulletin of the Atomic Scientists,* May/June 2000.

_____, "Top Air Force Leaders to Get Briefed on Serbia Air War Report," *Defense Daily,* June 13, 2000.

Aubin, Stephen P., "*Newsweek* and the 14 Tanks," *Air Force Magazine,* July 2000.

Barber, Ben, "Milosevic May Have Been Spooked into Leaving Kosovo," *Washington Times,* July 20, 1999.

Barry, John, and Evan Thomas, "The Kosovo Cover-Up," *Newsweek,* May 15, 2000.

Beaumont, Peter, and Patrick Westover, "Leaks in NATO—and Plan Bravo Minus," *London Sunday Observer,* July 18, 1999.

Becker, Elizabeth, "Kosovo Talks Break Down As Serbs Balk over Details; NATO Will Step Up Bombing," *New York Times,* June 7, 1999.

Bennett, Philip, and Steve Coll, "NATO Warplanes Jolt Yugoslav Power Grid," *Washington Post,* May 25, 1999.

"BETA Examines Milosevic's Kosovo Options," BETA, March 4, 1999, *FBIS* translated text, FTS19990304000223.

"BETA Sees Belgrade Profiting from Strikes," BETA, March 18, 1999, *FBIS* translated text, FTS1999031800546.

Biserko, Sonya, "Comment: The Belgrade Stranglehold," *Institute for War and Peace Reporting*, February 11, 2000, http://iwpr.vs4. cerbernet.co.uk/index.pl?archive/bcr/bcr_20000211_3_eng.txt.

Block, Robert, "Belgrade's Papers Are Filled with Broadsides Aimed at Milosevic in Wake of Kosovo Accord," *Wall Street Journal*, June 7, 1999.

_____, "Struggle for Milosevic's Political Life Begins," *Wall Street Journal*, June 11, 1999.

Boarov, Dimititrije, and Christopher Bennett, "The Economic Cost of Mr. Milosevic," *Institute for War and Peace Reporting*, June 16, 1999, http://iwpr.vs4.cerbernet.co.uk/index.pl?archive/bcr/bcr_19990616_1_eng.txt.

Bohlen, Celestine, "'Don't Push Us,' Yeltsin Warns West on Balkans," *New York Times*, April 10, 1999.

Bonner, Raymond, "Oil Flowing to Yugoslavia Despite NATO's Exertions," *New York Times*, May 25, 1999.

Booth, William, "Bombs Broke Hearts and Minds: In Yugoslavia, Lasting Damage Will Be Psychological," *Washington Post*, July 17, 1999.

Borowiec, Andrew, "Milosevic Family and Cronies Have Billions Stashed Abroad," *Washington Times*, June 3, 1999.

_____, "U.N. Sees Yugoslavia Taking Years to Recover," *Washington Times*, October 7, 2000.

Boucher, Richard, U.S. Department of State Press Briefing, January 2, 2001.

Bremmer, Charles, "NATO 'Spy' Says France Used Him," *London Times*, June 9, 2000.

Briefing and press conference on the Kosovo Strike Assessment by General Wesley K. Clark, Supreme Allied Commander, Europe, and Brigadier General John Corley, Chief, Kosovo Munitions

Effectiveness Assessment Team, NATO Headquarters, September 16, 1999.

Casey, Lee, and David Rivkin, "Clinton's Worst Folly," *Washington Times*, January 9, 2001.

Central Intelligence Agency, *The World Factbook 1998.*

Chernomyrdin, Viktor, "Impossible to Talk Peace with Bombs Falling," *Washington Post*, May 27, 1999.

Ciric, Aleksander, "Comment: It's a Serbian Thing," *Institute for War and Peace Reporting*, April 15, 1999, http://iwpr.vs4.cerbernet. co.uk/index.pl?archive/bcr/bcr_19990415_1_eng.txt.

"Clark Looks Back on Kosovo Conflict," *Defense Week*, August 23, 1999.

"Clinton's Remarks in Defense of Military Intervention in Balkans," *New York Times*, May 14, 1999.

Cohen, Roger, "In a Breach, German Party Backs 'Limited Halt' in Kosovo Air War," *New York Times*, May 14, 1999.

_____, "Milosevic's Vision of Glory Unleashed Decades of Ruin," *New York Times*, July 2, 1999.

Colenco Power Engineering Ltd., "Electricity and Heating in the Federal Republic of Yugoslavia," U.N. Office for the Coordination of Humanitarian Affairs, Belgrade, September 20, 1999.

Cowell, Alan, "It's a Wonder This Alliance Is Unified," *New York Times*, April 25, 1999.

Daalder, Ivo H., and Michael E. O'Hanlon, *Winning Ugly: NATO's War to Save Kosovo*, Washington, D.C.: Brookings Institution Press, 2000.

Dannreuther, Roland, "Escaping the Enlargement Trap in NATO-Russian Relations," *Survival*, Winter 1999.

Dascalu, Adrian, "Agreement Brings Relief for Yugoslav Citizenry," *Washington Times*, June 4, 1999.

de Borchgrave, Arnaud, "We Are Willing to Defend Our Rights," *Washington Times*, May 1, 1999.

_____, "Serbs Concede Making Big Miscalculation," *Washington Times*, June 11, 1999.

"The Dead Don't Care About Kosovo," *Institute for War and Peace Reporting*, June 3, 1999, http://iwpr.vs4.cerbernet.co.uk/index. pl?archive/bcr/bcr_19990603_4_eng.txt.

Dinmore, Guy, "NATO Destroys Major Bridge," *Washington Post*, April 4, 1999.

_____, "Daily Life in Belgrade Teeters Under Strikes," *Washington Post*, April 5, 1999.

Dobbs, Michael, "Serbs Bull's-Eyes Defy, Mock NATO," *Washington Post*, April 9, 1999.

_____, "NATO Bombing Campaign Wounds Milosevic's Political Enemies," *Washington Post*, April 13, 1999.

_____, "Allied Strike Denounced as 'Attempt on Milosevic,'" *Washington Post*, April 23, 1999.

_____, "Despairing Serbs Struggle for Survival," *Washington Post*, reprinted in *Manchester Guardian Weekly*, June 27, 1999.

Doder, Dusko, and Louise Branson, *Milosevic, Portrait of a Tyrant*, New York: The Free Press, 1999.

Drozdiak, William, "The Kosovo Peace Deal: How It Happened," *Washington Post*, June 6, 1999.

Erlanger, Steven, "NATO Raids Send Notice to Milosevic: Businesses He Holds Are Fair Game," *New York Times*, April 22, 1999.

_____, "Diplomat Says Serbs Want Some Albanians in Kosovo," *New York Times*, April 25, 1999.

_____, "A Liberal Threatens Milosevic with Street Protests," *New York Times*, April 27, 1999.

_____, "Yugoslav Politicians Carefully Maneuver for Day Milosevic Is Gone," *New York Times*, May 21, 1999.

_____, "Belgrade's People Still Defiant, but Deeply Weary," *New York Times*, May 24, 1999.

_____, "Dozens of Civilians Are Killed As NATO Air Strikes Go Awry," *New York Times*, June 1, 1999.

_____, "Fruit of Miscalculation," *New York Times*, June 4, 1999.

_____, "In Milosevic's Government, Resignation over Pact, Confidence in His Strength," *New York Times*, June 5, 1999.

_____, "Ignoring Scars, Milosevic Is Stubbornly Pressing On," *New York Times*, October 31, 1999.

Federal Republic of Yugoslavia, Agreement on Sub-Regional Arms Control, Information on the Army of Yugoslavia, Annual Data Exchange, valid as of January 1, 1999.

_____, Information on Armaments Limited by the Agreement on Sub-Regional Arms Control in Federal Republic of Yugoslavia, entry into force January 1, 2000.

Final Report to the Prosecutor by the Committee Established to Review the NATO Bombing Campaign Against the Federal Republic of Yugoslavia, http://www.un.org/icty/pressreal/nato061300.htm.

Fisher, Ian, "Aided by NATO Bombing, Rebels Position Themselves to Become Kosovo's New Army," *New York Times*, June 9, 1999.

Fisk, Robert, "NATO 'Deliberately Attacked Civilians in Serbia.'" *The Independent Digital* (UK), June 7, 2000, http://www.independent.co.u...Europe/2000-06.

Fletcher, Philippa, "NATO Air Strikes Lead to Tough Times for Serbs," *Washington Times*, May 12, 1999.

Gall, Carlotta, "No Water, Power, Phone: A Serbian City's Trials," *New York Times*, May 4, 1999.

_____, "Embassy Attack Followed by Defiance Toward NATO," *New York Times*, May 10, 1999.

_____, "Women Protest Draftees' Kosovo Duty," *New York Times*, May 20, 1999.

_____, "Protests Are Resumed by Families of Yugoslav Reservists Ordered Back to Duty in Kosovo," *New York Times*, May 25, 1999.

_____, "Serbs Raise an Obstacle to Return of Refugees," *New York Times*, June 9, 1999.

Gee, Marcus, "Jokes, Tears Help Serbs Cope with Raids," *Washington Times*, June 2, 1999.

"Gen. Pavkovic Threatens to Take Serb Army Back to Kosovo," Belgrade *Tanjug* in English, June 13, 1999, *FBIS* translated text, FTS199906130000629.

Gertz, Bill, "Cohen, Shelton See Victory in Kosovo Without a Treaty: Bombing Can Reduce Enemy Power to That of KLA," *Washington Times*, April 16, 1999.

_____, "Clinton Has Plans to Unseat Milosevic," *Washington Times*, June 30, 1999.

Gordon, Michael R., "U.S. Warns Russia: Don't Provide Help to Serbian Military," *New York Times*, April 10, 1999.

_____, "Kremlin Says NATO As Well As Serbs Must Compromise," *New York Times*, April 27, 1999

_____, "Allied Air Chief Stresses Hitting Belgrade Sites," *New York Times*, May 13, 1999.

Gordon, Michael R., and Eric Schmitt, "Shift in Targets Let NATO Jets Tip the Balance," *New York Times*, June 5, 1999.

Gordy, Eric D., *The Culture of Power in Serbia*, University Park, PA: Pennsylvania State University Press, 1999.

_____, "Why Milosevic Still?" *Current History*, March 2000.

Graham, Bradley, "Missiles Hit State TV, Residence of Milosevic," *Washington Post*, April 23, 1999.

Harden, Blaine, "A Long Struggle That Led Serb Leaders to Back Down," *New York Times*, June 6, 1999.

"Harsh Reality Under the Bombs," *Institute for War and Peace Reporting,* June 3, 1999, http://iwpr.vs4.cerbernet.co.uk/index. pl?archive/bcr/bcr_19990603_3_eng.txt.

Headquarters United States Air Force, *Initial Report: The Air War over Serbia*, no date.

Hedges, Chris, "Angry Serbs Hear a New Explanation: It's All Russia's Fault," *New York Times,* July 16, 1999.

Hess, Pamela, "Pentagon Takes Strong Exception to UN Criminal Court," *United Press International,* June 12, 2000.

Hilsum, Lindsay (*London Observer*), "Serbs Protest Kosovo Fighting," *Washington Times*, May 24, 1999.

Hosmer, Stephen T., *Psychological Effects of U.S. Air Operations in Four Wars 1941–1991: Lessons for U.S. Commanders*, Santa Monica: RAND, MR-576-AF, 1996.

Human Rights Watch, "New Figures on Civilian Deaths in Kosovo War," February 7, 2000, http://www.hrw.org/press/2000/02/nato207.htm.

_____, "Summary, Civilian Deaths in the NATO Air Campaign," February 7, 2000, http://www.hrw.org/reports/2000/nato/Natbm200.htm.

International Institute for Strategic Studies, *The Military Balance 1999–2000*, London: Oxford University Press, 1999.

Interview with Viktor Chernomyrdin, PBS *Frontline,* "War in Europe," February 22, 2000, http://www.pbs.org/wgbh/pages/frontline/shows/kosovo/interviews.

Interview with Secretary of Defense William Cohen, PBS *Frontline*, "War in Europe," February 22, 2000, http://www.pbs.org/wgbh/pages/frontline/shows/kosovo/interviews.

Interview with Richard Holbrooke, PBS *Frontline*, "War in Europe," February 22, 2000, http://www.pbs.org/wgbh/pages/frontline/shows/kosovo/interviews.

Interview with Slobodan Milosevic, Belgrade Palma Television, December 12, 2000, *FBIS* translated text, EUP20001214000131.

Interview with General Klaus Naumann, Chairman of NATO's Military Committee, PBS *Frontline*, "War in Europe," February 22, 2000, http://www.pbs.org/wgbh/pages/frontline/shows/kosovo/interviews.

Interview with General Pavkovic, PBS *Frontline*, "War in Europe," February 22, 2000, http://www.pbs.org/wgbh/pages/frontline/shows/kosovo/interviews.

Interview with Lieutenant General Michael Short, PBS *Frontline*, "War in Europe," February 22, 2000, http://www.pbs.org/wgbh/pages/frontline/shows/kosovo/interviews.

Interview with Lieutenant General Michael Short, Wright-Patterson AFB, Dayton, Ohio, February 2, 2000.

Interview with Strobe Talbott, PBS *Frontline*, "War in Europe,"February 22, 2000, http://www.pbs.org/wgbh/pages/frontline/shows/kosovo/interviews.

Interviews with General Short, General Pavkovic, and President Ahtisaari, "Moral Combat: NATO at War," transcript of a BBC2 Special, March 12, 2000, http://news6.thdo.bbc.co.uk/hi/english/static/audio%5Fvideo/programmes/panorama/transcripts/transcript%5F112%5F03%5F00.bxt.

Isachenkov, Vladimir, "Russian General Openly Questions NATO Deal on Kosovo," *Washington Times*, June 10, 1999.

Jackson, Lieutenant General Sir Mike, "KFOR: The Inside Story," *RUSI Journal*, February 2000.

Jahn, George, "Strikes Destroy Novi Sad's Last Bridge," *Washington Times*, April 26, 1999.

_____, "Desperation Takes Over Belgrade," Associated Press, May 1, 1999.

Joint Task Force Noble Anvil, *Psychological Operations Support to Allied Force*, July 14, 1999.

Judah, Tim, *Kosovo: War and Revenge*, New Haven, CT: Yale University Press, 2000.

Kesic, Obrad, "Serbian Roulette," *Current History*, March 1998.

"The KLA: Braced to Defend and Control," *Jane's Intelligence Review*, April 1999.

"Kosovo and Politics in FRY—A New Round Starts," BETA Commentary, June 9, 1999, *FBIS-EEU*-1999-0609.

"The Kosovo Crisis After May 1997," Select Committee on Foreign Affairs, Fourth Report, House of Commons, May 23, 2000, http://www.parliament.the.stationary.off.../pa/cm/199900/cmselect/cmfaff/28/2808/html.

"The Kosovo Talks: Holbrooke as Last Chance," BETA, March 11, 1999, BETA Commentary, *FBIS* transcribed text, FTS19990311000225.

"Kosovo: The Military Campaign," Select Committee on Foreign Affairs, Fourth Report, House of Commons, May 23, 2000, http://www.parliament.the.stationary.off.../pa/cm/199900/cmselect/cmfaff/28/2812/html.

"Kosovo Update," *New York Times*, June 2, 1999.

Kusovac, Zoran, "Croat General to Lead KLA as Part of Reorganization," *Jane's Defence Weekly*, May 12, 1999.

Letters to the editor from John Barry and Stephen P. Aubin, *Air Force Magazine*, August 2000.

Levitin, Oleg, "Inside Moscow's Kosovo Muddle," *Survival*, Spring 2000.

Lust, Larry J., "Kosovo Campaign Logistics," ECJ4 Log Briefing, Headquarters, United States European Command, July 1999.

Malcolm, Noel, *Kosovo: A Short History*, New York: Harper Perennial, 1999.

Marshall, Tyler, and Richard Boudreaux, "How an Uneasy Alliance Prevailed," *Los Angeles Times*, June 6, 1999.

Memorandum by the Foreign and Commonwealth Office, "Kosovo: History of the Crisis," Select Committee on Foreign Affairs, Fourth Report, Minutes of Evidence, House of Commons, May 23, 2000, http://www.parliament.the_stationary_off.../pa/cm199900/cmsel ect/cmfaff/28/9111803.html.

Mertus, Julie A., *Kosovo: How Myths and Truths Started a War*, Berkeley and Los Angeles: University of California Press, 1999.

"Minister: Damage Inflicted on Media Exceeds $1 Billion," BETA, May 30, 1999, *FBIS* translated text, FBIS19990530000788.

Myers, Steven Lee, "All in Favor of This Target, Say Yes, Si, Oui, Ja," *New York Times*, April 25, 1999.

_____, "U.S. Military Chiefs Firm: No Ground Force for Kosovo," *New York Times*, June 3, 1999.

"National Unity: Utter Exhaustion," *Institute for War and Peace Reporting*, May 21, 1999, http://iwpr.vs4.cerbernet.co.uk/index. pl?archive/bcr/bcr_19990521_2_eng.txt.

NATO Headquarters, *Operation Allied Force Updates*, May 30–May 31, 1999.

_____, *Operation Allied Force Updates*, May 22–June 2, 1999.

NATO Press Release S-1(99)62, April 23, 1999.

"NATO's Game of Chicken," *Newsweek*, July 26, 1999.

Naudet, Jean Baptiste, "'We're All Going Crazy Here, We're on Pills,'" *Le Monde*, May 25, 1999, reprinted in *Manchester Guardian Weekly*, June 6, 1999.

"Opinion Poll: 78.5% of Citizens Do Not Expect Air Strikes," BETA, March 18, 1999, *FBIS* translated excerpt, FTS19990318001456.

OSCE, *Kosovo, As Seen, As Told*, December 1999, http://www.osce. org/kosovo/reports.html.

PBS *Frontline*, "War in Europe," a Kosovo chronology, February 22, 2000, http://www.pbs.org/wgbh/pages/frontline/shows/kosovo/ etc/cron.html.

Perry, Duncan, "Macedonia's Quest for Security and Stability," *Current History*, March 2000.

Pickering, Thomas, Undersecretary of State for Political Affairs, Testimony Before the House International Relations Committee, May 13, 1999.

Press conference by Secretary General Dr. Javier Solana and SACEUR General Wesley Clark, March 25, 1999.

Press statement by James P. Rubin, spokesman, U.S. Department of State, Office of the Spokesman, April 6, 1999.

Putnik, Milena, "Broken Bridges, Disrupted Lives," *Institute for War and Peace Reporting*, May 4, 1999, http://iwpr.vs4.cerbernet. co.uk/index.pl?archive/bcr/bcr_19990504_1_eng.txt.

"Radical Leader Says Russian Plan Fits with Yugoslav Principles," Belgrade *Borba*, May 31, 1999, *FBIS* translated text, FTS19990531001432.

Radio-Television Serbia broadcast by Lieutenant General Pavkovic, June 11, 1999, *FBIS* translated text, FTS19990611001741.

Rambouillet Agreement, *Interim Agreement for Peace and Self-Government in Kosovo*.

RFE/RL Balkan Report, Vol. 2, No. 48, December 9, 1998.

Ribnikar, Darko, "Washington Is Opposing Peace," *Politika*, May 31, 1999, *FBIS* translated text, FTS19990601000520.

"Rival Frustrations," *Institute for War and Peace Reporting*, July 13, 1999, http://iwpr.vs4.cerbernet.co.uk/index.pl?archive/bcr/bcr_19990713_3_eng.txt.

Robbins, Carla Anne, Tom Ricks, and Robert Block, "Envoys Start Kosovo Talks in Belgrade," *Wall Street Journal*, June 3, 1999.

Sands, David R., "Yugoslavia Capitulates; Air War May Stop Today, Accord Meets NATO's Demands," *Washington Times*, June 10, 1999.

Scarborough, Rowan, "Bombing Utilities Could Backfire, Experts Warn," *Washington Times*, May 25, 1999.

Scheffer, David J., "Deterrence of War Crimes in the 21st Century," address to the Twelfth Annual U.S. Pacific Command International Military Operations and Law Conference, Honolulu, Hawaii, February 23, 1999.

_____, "Evolution of U.S. Policy Toward the International Criminal Court," address at American University, Washington, D.C., September 14, 2000.

Schmitt, Eric, "Hundreds of Yugoslav Troops said to Desert," *New York Times*, May 20, 1999.

Schmitt, Michael N., and Major Peter J. Richards, U.S. Air Force, "Into Uncharted Waters: The International Criminal Court," *Naval War College Review*, Winter 2000.

"Seeds of Discontent," *Institute for War and Peace Reporting*, May 25, 1999, http://iwpr.vs4.cerbernet.co.uk/index.pl?archive/bcr/bcr_19990525_2_eng.txt.

Senate Committee on Armed Services hearing on "Lessons Learned from Military Operations and Relief Efforts in Kosovo," October 21, 1999.

"Shoot First, Live Longer," *Institute for War and Peace Reporting*, July 21, 1999, http://iwpr.vs4.cerbernet.co.uk/index.pl?archive/bcr/bcr_19990721_3_eng.txt.

Smith, R. Jeffrey, "The Hunt for Yugoslav Riches," *Washington Post*, March 11, 2001.

Smith, R. Jeffrey, and Peter Finn, "How Milosevic Lost His Grip," *Washington Post*, October 15, 2000.

"Special Defense Department Briefing on Serb Withdrawal from Kosovo and NATO Bombing Pause," *Federal News Service*, June 10, 1999.

Stabile, Alberto, interview with Viktor Chernomyrdin, June 10, 1999, as reported in *Rome La Republica*, June 11, 1999, *FBIS* translated text, FTS19990611000441.

Statement by President Clinton to the nation, March 24, 1999.

Statement of Prime Minister Tony Blair before the House of Commons, March 23, 1999, quoted in *Kosovo: The Military Campaign*, Select Committee on Foreign Affairs, Fourth Report, House of Commons, May 23, 2000, http://www.parliament.the.stationary.off.../pa/cm/199900/cmselect/cmfaff/28/2812.html.

Stojanovic, Dusan, "Yugoslav Leader Rebuffs U.N. Tribunal Prosecutor," *Washington Times*, January 24, 2001.

Text of President Clinton's December 31 statement authorizing the United States to sign the Treaty on the International Criminal Court, *New York Times*, January 1, 2001.

Thomas, Robert, *The Politics of Serbia in the 1990s*, New York: Columbia University Press, 1999.

"Two Months of Air Campaign Against Yugoslavia," BETA , May 27, 1999, *FBIS* translated text, FTS19990527001145.

U.K. Ministry of Defence, *Kosovo: Lessons from the Crisis*, June 2000.

United Nations Environment Programme (UNEP) and United Nations Centre for Human Settlements (UNCHS) Balkan Task Force, *BTF—Hot Spot Report Bor*, 1999.

United Nations, Office for the Coordination of Humanitarian Affairs, Humanitarian Risk Analysis No. 4, Federal Republic of Yugoslavia, OCHA Belgrade, October 1, 1999.

United Nations Resolution 1244 (1999), adopted by the Security Council at its 4011th meeting on June 10, 1999.

United Nations Security Council, letter dated June 15, 1999, from the Secretary-General addressed to the president of the Security Council. Enclosure: military-technical agreement between the international security force (KFOR) and the governments of the Federal Republic of Yugoslavia and the Republic of Serbia, June 9, 1999.

United States Energy Information Administration, "Serbia and Montenegro," June 1999, http://www.eia.doe.gov/emeu/cabs/sermont.hmtl.

U.S. Department of Defense, Report to Congress, *Kosovo/Operation Allied Force After-Action Report,* January 31, 2000.

U.S. Department of Defense news briefing by Brigadier General John Corley, May 8, 2000.

U.S. GAO, *Balkans Security: Current and Projected Factors Affecting Regional Stability,* Briefing Report, GAO/NSIAD-00-125BR, July 24, 2000.

Vasovic, Milenko, "Serbia's Incredible Reconstruction," *Institute for War and Peace Reporting,* February 11, 2000, http://iwpr.vs4. cerbernet.co.uk/index.pl?archive/bcr/bcr_20000211_4_eng.txt.

V.I.P. Daily News Report 1465, March 19, 1999.

_____, *1467,* March 23, 1999.

_____, *1471,* March 27, 1999.

_____, *1510,* May 20, 1999.

_____, *1512,* May 24, 1999.

_____, *1515,* May 27, 1999.

_____, *1517,* May 31, 1999.

, *1518,* June 1, 1999.

_____, *1521,* June 4, 1999.

_____, *1525,* June 10, 1999.

Watson, Paul, "Despite NATO Rhetoric, Rebels May Be Ultimate Beneficiaries of Air War," *Los Angeles Times,* May 12, 1999.

Weller, Marc, "The Rambouillet Conference on Kosovo," *International Affairs,* Vol. 75, No. 2, April 1999.

Whitney, Craig R., "Confident in Their Bombs, Allies Still Plan for Winter," *New York Times,* May 5, 1999.

_____, "NATO Presses Attack, and Plans for Peace," *New York Times,* June 2, 1999, p. A13.

_____, "Allies Say Bombing Will Intensify After Serbs Balk at Signing Pullout Proposal," *New York Times*, June 7, 1999.

Wines, Michael, "Russia and NATO, Split over Kosovo, Agree to Renew Relations," *New York Times*, February 17, 2000.

Yeltsin, Boris, *Midnight Diaries*, translated by Catherine A. Fitzpatrick, New York: Public Affairs, 2000.

Yugoslav Army Supreme Command Headquarters—Information Service, "Foreign Correspondents in Yugoslavia," Press Center, April 12, 1999.

_____, "Industrial or Manufacturing Facilities Demolished or Damaged by the NATO Aggression," Press Center, May 22, 1999.

_____, "Forces of Dark," Press Center, May 28, 1999.

_____, "55 Bridges Demolished," Press Center, June 6, 1999.

_____, "774 Hours of Air Raids in Belgrade," Press Center, June 17, 1999.

_____, Daily Review 26, "Statement by the Head of the Supreme Command HQ, Lieutenant General Dragoljub Ojdanic," Press Center, April 28, 1999.

_____, Daily Review 28, "Statement by Colonel Milivoje Novkovic, Head of the Supreme Command HQ Information Service," Press Center, May 1, 1999.

_____, Daily Review 49, "NATO Raids on Manufacturing and Civilian Facilities on May 21st and in the Night Between May 21st and 22nd, 1999," Press Center, May 22, 1999.

_____, Daily Review 50, "NATO Raids on Manufacturing and Civilian Facilities on May 22nd and in the Night Between May 22nd and 23rd, 1999," Press Center, Press Center, May 23, 1999.

_____, Daily Review 54, "NATO Raids on Civilian and Manufacturing Facilities on May 26th and in the Night Between May 26th and 27th, 1999," Press Center, May 27, 1999.

_____, Daily Review 58, "NATO Raids on Manufacturing and Civilian Facilities on May 30th and in the Night Between May 30th and 31st, 1999," Press Center, May 31, 1999.

_____, Daily Review 59, "NATO Raids on Manufacturing Facilities on May 31st and in the Night Between May 31st and June 1st, 1999," Press Center, June 1, 1999.

_____, Daily Review 68, "NATO Raids on Manufacturing and Civilian Facilities on June 9th and in the Night Between June 9th and 10th, 1999," Press Center, June 10, 1999.

"Yugoslav President Slobodan Milosevic's Address to the Nation," Belgrade *Borba*, June 10, 1999, *FBIS* translated text, FTS19990610001656.

Zivanovic, N., "Mirosinka Dinkic—An Economist Talks About Government Employment Programs: 'The Solution Is Not on the Farm,'" Belgrade *Blic*, June 7, 1999, *FBIS* translated text, FTS199906080001674.